SEEING JESUS IN EVERY BOOK OF THE BIBLE

THE WHOLE BIBLE DEVOTIONAL

Melissa A. McLaughlin

Fort Washington, PA 19034

The Whole Bible Devotional: Seeing Jesus in Every Book of the Bible
Published by CLC Publications

USA: P.O. Box 1449, Fort Washington, PA 19034
www.clcpublications.com

UK: Kingsway CLC Trust
Unit 5, Glendale Avenue, Sandycroft, Flintshire, CH5 2QP
www.equippingthechurch.com

Printed in the United States of America

ISBN (paperback): 978-1-61958-400-6
ISBN (ebook): 978-1-61958-401-3

Italics in Scripture quotations are the emphasis of the author.

PRAISE FOR

THE WHOLE BIBLE DEVOTIONAL

"As I read each page, I felt like I was reading God's Word with a friend. The personal experiences, the Scripture readings, and the heartfelt prayers allowed me to glean from God's Word without being overwhelmed. This is a wonderful book to share with others. Great to give as a gift."

— Melissa Henderson
Award-Winning Author

"The structure of this devotional is genius. Summarizing each Bible book through key scriptures and guiding us through insightful prayers that instruct and encourage, McLaughlin makes the Bible more accessible than ever, always pointing the reader back to the main point—Jesus. In a sea of devotionals, this is the one to pick up if you're looking for simple, effective, and Spirit-breathed."

— Jessie Mattis
Award-Winning Author, *Power Up*

"*The Whole Bible Devotional* reminds me of a preview to a good movie. Once you see the preview, you can't wait to see the movie! Each day's devotional provides the cliffhanger that will, in her words, "jump-start your prayers" and create within you "an ever-increasing measure of His Word, His Spirit, His truth, His passion, His grace, and His unending love." Melissa's invitation to join her in a prayerful walk through this devotional is actually an invitation to walk with Jesus through the whole Bible. All 66 books, every word, cover to cover, from Genesis to Revelation."

— Reverend Daniel Alford
Interim Pastor, Macedonia Ministries
Past President/Spiritual Advisor, Kingdom Road Warriors Motorcycle Ministry

"Melissa McLaughlin's *The Whole Bible Devotional* gives hope to those who've struggled to read the Bible and understand God's big picture. She outlines the Old and New Testaments, draws wisdom from each book, and connects Genesis to Revelation—connections too often lost in read-the-Bible-in-a-year programs. Melissa weaves together the separate pieces of 66 Bible books into a beautiful quilt of God's love, mercy, and grace. A wonderful tool for new believer and veteran Christ-follower alike!"

— Nancy E. Head
Award-Winning Author, *Restoring the Shattered*

"A delightful devotional, full of wisdom and insight, showing us how Jesus is woven throughout the Bible. Melissa laces encouragement into each chapter and masterfully points us back to Christ. A great resource for Sunday school classes, Bible study groups, or individuals. You will find yourself revisiting this book often to help deepen your faith."

— Yvonne M. Morgan
Christian Author, *Gypsy For God*

"An extraordinary, deeply helpful book in today's fast-paced world, capturing the essence of God's Word and God's love from every single book in the Bible. The Bible can seem daunting for people; even those who manage to read through it sometimes have difficulty grasping the simple, universal message of God's perfect, glorious plan. This book is a solution, masterfully weaving complexities with simplicity and enabling us all to understand the truth of the Bible, which is God's love letter to us all."

— Jessica Brodie
Award-Winning Journalist, Author, Editor, and Writing Coach

"If you've ever wondered how to capture a big-picture understanding of the Bible, this is the book for you. Melissa McLaughlin guides us on a journey from Genesis to Revelation, weaving the Old Testament to the New Testament and capturing Jesus all along the way. Melissa's writing is refreshingly savored with humility and vulnerability. My favorite aspect of this devotional is Melissa's deep love for her Lord and Savior, Jesus Christ, as the key focus. What a unique devotional about the Bible that is sure to reach your heart and renew your desire for God's Word!"

— Karen Friday
Pastor's wife, Christian Speaker, Blogger, and Published Author
in Christian Anthologies and Devotional Books

Melissa McLaughlin is the perfect person to give us *The Whole Bible Devotional: Seeing Jesus in Every Book of the Bible*. She is able to effectively and inspiringly point out Jesus in every book of the Bible because of her genuine, loving relationship with Jesus. Jesus is not hidden from her sight, and her devotional will help readers see him more clearly, too.

Rev. Dr. Ed Crenshaw
Senior Pastor, Victory Church, Philadelphia
Author, *Invite Your Neighbor, Change the World*

I dedicate this book to
my husband and my children.

My prayer for you, dear reader:

Heavenly Father, thank You for the person reading this right now. Thank You for sending Jesus to die for their sins, so they could have eternal life in heaven and experience Your love. Holy Spirit, shine into this person's soul with the light of Your truth and grace. Let these words come alive as they read. Let this person's soul be renewed and strengthened. Let each one be changed as they know more of Jesus' holiness, mercy, and unending love. In Jesus' name, Amen.

Contents

PART 1
An Overview of the Bible

1 First Things First 11

2 How Does a Bible Overview Help? 15

3 Bible Overview 19

PART 2
Sixty-Six Readings, Genesis to Revelation

Old Testament Scriptures and Prayers............... 31–87

New Testament Scriptures and Prayers 89–132

Appendix A: A One-Year Bible Reading Plan 133

Appendix B: Bible Reading Guidelines................. 139

Appendix C: Bible-Based Prayer 147

Acknowledgments 153

PART 1

An Overview of the Bible

1

First Things First

Faith comes by hearing and hearing by the Word of God.

Romans 10:17, NKJV

HAVE YOU EVER tried to read the whole Bible only to give up partway through? Have you ever made it through the Bible only to realize by the end that you couldn't connect the dots? You are not alone.

I was sixteen years old when I first read the Bible from Genesis to Revelation. Though I didn't fully grasp everything, accomplishing this daunting goal felt exhilarating. I loved Jesus, and I yearned to know Him through His Word. Reading the Bible brought me closer to my Savior.

As the years passed, God blessed me with a loving husband and three wonderful children. We faithfully attended church and desired to grow in our Christian faith. When my kids reached their teen years, it seemed the perfect time to read through the Bible together. So, one afternoon, I invited my teens to tackle this challenge with me. They responded positively, and we jumped right in.

As you may have guessed, it all fell apart.

Maybe life is busier now; maybe smartphones make it too easy to locate sound-bite answers with the touch of a finger; maybe we are too distracted. I don't know. One thing I do know is that even with the best of intentions, we never made it through. After an enthusiastic start, we sputtered, restarted, and finally gave up.

I felt trapped by defeat. Negative words swirled in my mind: *quitter*; *weak*; *uncommitted.* I had failed my kids and my Savior. I made time to finish other important tasks; why couldn't I complete this one? Where were my priorities?

I knew the benefits of God's Word. Like a divine lifeline, Bible reading refueled my mind and renewed my spirit. I deeply regretted not developing this spiritual asset with my family.

Furthermore, I knew that reading only bits and pieces of the Bible had, in the past, caused me to stumble, and led me to misunderstand and misrepresent God. I have learned the hard way that to know our Savior fully, we need to know His Word in full.

Since that unsuccessful attempt to read the Bible with my kids, a tugging on my heart wouldn't let go. That pull encouraged me to write a Bible study to help believers understand the entire Bible in a manageable way.

Help Is on the Way!

For those who don't have time to read the whole Bible, or for those who have read through the Bible but don't understand how it all fits together, this book is for you.

The Whole Bible Devotional provides a format for you to read representative passages of every book of the Bible and see Jesus woven throughout. *The Whole Bible Devotional* begins with a brief, nonacademic Bible overview to lay the foundation for God's redemption plan through Christ.

- The overview offers a snapshot of the overarching theme of the Bible: Jesus Christ. From beginning to end, Jesus Christ is the golden thread tying each book together. You will appreciate the entire biblical narrative as God's rescue story. Page by page, you will see God restoring humanity to a right relationship with Himself.
- The Bible overview is followed by sixty-six readings of Scripture and prayer. These readings are unique. Unlike traditional daily devotionals, the Scripture texts are taken from the content found in each book of the Bible. Therefore, some readings are longer than others.
- Through the sixty-six short readings from every book of the Bible, you will gain a better knowledge of the Bible as a whole. You will also view God's salvation plan through Christ, unfolding book by book from Genesis to Revelation.
- Each Bible excerpt is paired with a corresponding prayer to ignite your faith and deepen your love for the Lord. Experience new spiritual vitality through Scripture readings and prayers that personally engage your heart with the Bible.
- In just sixty-six readings, you will obtain a big picture of the Bible.

May these Scriptures and prayers jump-start your prayers. May we join together across miles, across time, and across hearts as we grow in the grace and knowledge of Jesus Christ. May we be filled with an ever-increasing measure of His Word, His Spirit, His truth, His passion, His grace, and His unending love. And may we know and love Him more.

This is a life-changing endeavor. Join me now in a prayerful walk through *The Whole Bible Devotional.*

2

How Does a Bible Overview Help?

A WALK IN THE woods nourishes my soul like nothing else. Tall trees with deep-rooted strength display delicate leaves that whisper in the wind. Earthy smells from the rich soil enfold us. Woodland creatures scamper about. The stillness of the forest offers a welcome retreat that soothes my spirit.

A Mountaintop View

A hiking trail we frequent affords a sacred place with breathtaking vistas. This trail ascends high atop a mountain. Near the pinnacle is a coveted spot where we pause and gaze through the treetops to the vast land below. In awe, we behold miles and miles of God's creation as far as the eye can see.

When we view the earth from high above, we gain a better sense of God's grandeur and glory. We see hills rolling along, seemingly forever. Tiny country roads wind through valleys. Farmers' green crops sing of their harvest.

We take in this massive scene all at once.

When standing on the mountain's summit, we acquire a bigger perspective of life, and even our problems assume their rightful, lesser place in our mind's eye.

A Bird's-Eye View of the Bible

Much like the mountaintop view, an aerial perspective of the Bible enables us to see it as a whole. Life's problems dim in light of God's greatness.

A Bible overview also lays the foundation for God's long-range plan. It provides a wide-angle lens to frame our thinking. Then, as each book of the Bible is read, we recall that panoramic view and see how each small piece fits into God's big story.

The Main Message of the Bible

As we step back and view the Bible holistically, it becomes clear that it contains one overarching theme, one main message. That message is Jesus Christ. Together, let us ponder God's story, *His*-story, and how we fit into His glorious redemption plan.

The Bible's major point is this: God sent Jesus to restore, redeem, and re-create all that is fallen and broken. The Old Testament points ahead to Christ. The New Testament points back, illuminating Jesus as the fulfillment of the Old Testament prophecies.

Both Old and New Testament Scriptures also predict the future and final pages of God's magnificent narrative. God's account moves from creation to re-creation through our Savior, Jesus Christ.

God rescued us from this world of sin and strife through Jesus Christ. May the wonder of this great truth seep into our souls.

Jesus Woven Through the Bible

There are countless textbooks written on the topic of Jesus as the unifying theme of the Bible. Many scholarly resources provide in-depth details on the subject.

With today's fast-paced schedules, most people do not have time to take on a heavy theological textbook. Therefore, my goal is to provide a simple, nonacademic overview of Jesus as the Bible's unifying message traced from beginning to end.

Through Jesus, God takes us . . .

- ***From rest to rest***—God created us to rest with Him in the Garden of Eden. When we rest in Jesus' finished work on the cross, our sins are forgiven, salvation is assured, and our lives culminate in the soul rest of all eternity.
- ***From image to image***—We are reminded that human beings were formed from the dust of the earth, made in God's image. Yet, in order to pay our sin debt, Jesus' human image was marred on the cross so He could redeem us. Graciously, even now believers are being made more and more into the image of Christ, the Man of heaven.
- ***From garden to garden***—We marvel at the beautiful paradise God prepared to share with humanity in the Garden of Eden. We grimace at Jesus enduring agonizing pain in the Garden of Gethsemane, facing imminent torment on the cross for our sins. His sacrifice brought our soul healing, so we may enjoy heaven's eternal garden.

God also takes us . . .

- ***From creation to new creation through Jesus Christ***—Through faith in Christ, God has made us brand new. Once born in the flesh and shaped by God's hand, we are now born again of His Spirit and indwelled by His Spirit. We are washed clean and adopted into His family. Daily, God is refining us to reflect the image of our Savior. One day, we will take on spiritual, imperishable bodies perfectly suited for the glory of heaven.

What an amazing transformation story!

Before stepping off to enjoy individual books of the Bible, let's pause and take in the full view of God's redemption plan through a Bible overview. Don't miss this wonderful vantage point. The view is incredible.

3

Bible Overview

The Old Testament

Laying the Foundation

The first five books of the Bible lay the foundation for everything that follows. Therefore, the content of these books requires greater attention.

In these foundational books, we discover answers to life's essential questions.

- Why do we exist?
- Where did we come from?
- Who are we?
- Where are we going?

Let's get started.

In the Beginning—Creation Begins

God, the Creator of the heavens and the earth, commissioned His wondrous plan in Genesis. "In the beginning, God created the heavens and the earth" (Gen. 1:1, ESV).

On the sixth day of creation, after He designed and set all matter into motion, God declared that His creation was very good (Gen. 1:31, ESV).

We picture God's handiwork. We envision a lush paradise in the Garden of Eden. Here God walked in sweet, unhindered communion with Adam and Eve. The first man and woman flourished in total trust and harmony: harmony with God, harmony with one another, and harmony with creation.

In Graeme Goldsworthy's book, *Gospel and Kingdom*,[1] God's kingdom is described as:

- God's people
- In God's place
- Under God's rule

God's abundant blessings are found only within His kingdom.

Here, in the Garden of Eden, God's kingdom is captured in portrait. Adam and Eve enjoyed perfect peace and blessing. God is the Creator and rightful ruler over His kingdom, and He is a good God.

So what went wrong?

The Fall

The fall of mankind occurred when Satan entered the scene, taking the form of a serpent. Satan, the father of lies and master of deception, employed his infamous battle tactics.

In the same manner as today:

- ***Satan twisted God's Word***: "Did God really say?" (Gen. 3:1, NIV).
- ***Satan cast doubt on the truth of God's Word***: "You will not surely die" (Gen. 3:4, ESV).

1 Graeme Goldsworthy, "Gospel and Kingdom," in *The Goldsworthy Trilogy* (Milton Keynes, UK: Paternoster, 2000), 54.

- ***Satan discredited God's character*:** "God knows . . . you will become like God" (Gen. 3:5, ESV), as if God was withholding a blessing from Adam and Eve.

Eve, and then Adam, disregarded God's Word and instead acted on Satan's words. They chose to disobey and rebel against the one rule and boundary God had established in the Garden of Eden.

Creation's Consequences

This rebellion and sin brought terrible consequences. God is the Creator of life, so to rebel against Him brings death.

- Death of their close relationship with God, for they were cast out of the Garden of Eden.
- Death of their trusting relationship with one another, for now, men and women would strive to rule over one another in ungodly ways.
- Degradation of their caretaking role in the earth, for now, they would eat only after great toil and hardship with the soil.

Their physical death would soon come as well, for God guarded the Tree of Life. Now, after the fall, they could no longer partake in eternal life.

Yet, even this was God's mercy. Who would want to live in this world of sin forever?

Foreshadowing Christ

Remarkably, in this moment of great loss and tremendous brokenness, God foretold a promised Redeemer.

- A Serpent-Slayer
- A Deliverer
- A Savior
- A King

An offspring of Eve, a human, would save them.

In God's own divine irony, from among those deceived by Satan at the beginning, would come One destined to crush Satan's head (Gen. 3:14–15, NIV).

Stunningly, right there in the shattered ruins of a once-lovely and radiant creation, God declared His plan for a new creation. How beautiful is the heart of God!

Saved by Grace Through Faith

God's redemption plan moved forward as He called Abraham. God told Abraham He would bless all peoples of the earth through Abraham's descendants, a nation set apart as God's special people (12:1–3, NIV).

Why was Abraham chosen? Not by Abraham's merit, but by God's grace.

When God told Abraham He would bless him with descendants as numerous as the stars, Abraham took God at His Word. Abraham believed God, and it was counted to him as righteousness (15:4–6, ESV). What does this mean?

God has always saved by grace. Beginning with Abraham, God saved by grace, through faith. Likewise, we are made righteous through our belief in Christ and our faith in His Word. The importance of grace and faith was made clear from the start. Seen here in Genesis, God's saving grace points ahead to Christ.

Salvation by Substitution

In the book of Exodus, we find God's people, the descendants of Abraham, now being called the Israelites. The Egyptians enslaved the Israelites. Pharaoh, the Egyptian leader, attempted to annihilate the Israelites by killing their newborn sons. However, God's plans would not be stopped, and God spared Moses.

Through Moses, God displayed His power to Pharaoh and requested the Israelites be released. Pharaoh only increased his cruelty and oppression toward the enslaved Israelites. In a final warning, God avowed the firstborn sons in the land would be killed.

God protected His people by directing the Israelites to sacrifice a lamb and cover their doorposts with its blood. Wherever blood marked the houses of faith, death passed over, and the people and their firstborn sons were saved. This event was the first Passover.

The sacrificial Passover lamb foreshadowed Christ.

Once again, the people were saved by grace through faith in God and His Word (Exod. 12).

At this time, God displayed the concept of salvation by substitution. Some biblical scholars refer to this as substitutionary atonement. A lamb was sacrificed in place of the people, and through this substitute, they were saved.

Atonement is not a word we typically use in conversation. A common definition of atonement is making amends or reparation for an injury or wrong. The biblical definition of atonement involves being reconciled back to God. The debt for our sins was covered, or paid for, by Christ's sacrifice. Our sin no longer alienates us from God. Atonement was made. We are one with Him. Though first introduced here at Passover, Christ now acts as our substitutionary atonement.

Salvation Includes Rescue and Victory

In one final triumphant miracle, God parted the Red Sea, and Moses led God's people out of their Egyptian bondage. God's people walked to the Promised Land on dry ground. Through this feat, God demonstrated salvation as both rescue and victory. They were not only rescued from slavery but also brought to the Promised Land.

Similarly, one day, Jesus' sacrifice would provide rescue and victory for us. Through the cross, Christ mercifully atoned for our sins and graciously opened the doors to heaven for all who believe. God poured out a double blessing of mercy and grace for the Israelites, just as He would for us through Christ.

God's Dwelling Place

God expressed His desire to dwell with His people later in the book of Exodus. God knew His people needed Him. God is our Creator, and He sustains us day by day. We are designed by God to know Him, love Him, worship Him, and be close to Him. Plain and simple, God loves us, and we need Him. The Israelites' love and need for God is still true for us today.

As a result, God guided the Israelites in the construction of the Tabernacle, a place of worship for the people to draw near to Him. The Tabernacle represented His presence in beauty, purity, and holiness. The Tabernacle's sacred elements also pointed ahead to Christ.

Yet, how could a holy God dwell among a sinful people? God cannot allow evil in His presence. If He did, He would cease to be good. God would not compromise His integrity. Therefore, the next step in God's redemption plan involved teaching His people about His Law and sacrifices for sin.

Understanding God's Law

God provided the Israelites with His laws of righteousness, recorded in Exodus, Leviticus, and Deuteronomy. These laws helped God's people understand His truth, holiness, goodness, righteousness, and justice. God is perfect, and His ways are perfect.

It is important to note that God's promises and the righteousness God imparted to Abraham came before the law. Additionally, God provided salvation from Egyptian slavery before the law.

The law was not intended to save. The law illustrates God's holiness, purity, and perfection. The law acts as a mirror so we can see our sin as it really is. With new clarity, we discern the wide chasm between our sinful selves and our holy God.

In short, the law . . .

- reveals God's standards,
- exposes our sin, and
- spotlights our need for a Savior.

A Perfect Sacrifice for Sin

In Leviticus, we also learn how sacrifices are required to atone for sin.

God instituted a system of sacrifices so His people could be made right before Him. Sacrifices were needed for the cleansing of sin. Sacrifices created a sanctified connection between a holy God and sinful people.

The sacrifice was serious. When we oppose the God of life through our sin, the result brings death. Therefore, a sacrifice to atone for sin involved death. The sacrifice required animal blood. Further, the sacrificial animals had to be perfect, without a spot or blemish.

Animal sacrifices were offered again and again for the atonement of sin because people sinned again and again. Animal sacrifices would never completely remove humanity's sin. Therefore, this sacrificial system emphasized our need for Christ.

Only a human sacrifice could fully atone for human sin. But not just any human. Only a perfect, sinless, spotless human could atone for humanity's sin.

Throughout the remainder of the Old Testament, Christ's advent is signaled, promised, and foretold. Each book anticipates the future Messiah.

The New Testament

The Savior Has Come—Creation Restored

When Jesus arrived as the Messiah in the New Testament, He fulfilled the Scriptures regarding His first coming. Jesus lived out God's perfection in the flesh. God's laws were upheld. Then Jesus willingly laid down His life. A human sacrifice, a perfect, spotless Lamb, was slain to atone for our sins.

The Old Testament teachings have come full circle. Reflecting Old Testament laws, Jesus is the perfect sacrifice for our sins, providing salvation by substitution. Like Abraham, in Christ we are saved by grace through faith.

Victory in Jesus

God has done it all and been faithful throughout! From the beginning, when creation was formed in all its glory, through the sin that separated us from our loving Creator, to the unimaginable, immeasurable price paid to redeem mankind.

What still awaits is the final re-creation that Jesus will bring forth in the new heaven and the new earth (Rev. 21:1–5).

God's grace is poured out to us through faith. We need only believe in the righteousness Jesus won for us through His life, death, burial, and resurrection.

Christ bought our salvation, arose from the grave, ascended into heaven, and sent His Holy Spirit to indwell the hearts of all who confess Him as Savior and Lord.

As we are filled with His Spirit and anchored in His Word, we are given divine power to overcome sin and grow in the holiness of God. Now, we seek to live out God's laws of goodness and righteousness, not to earn our salvation, but out of gratitude to our Savior, who earned salvation for us.

The Main Message of the Bible: Creation to New Creation

We go from creation to new creation through Jesus Christ, as individuals and as a Kingdom people. This is God's plan for all who believe and receive Christ as Savior and Lord. This is God's design for you and me.

How does this moment in time fit into God's big redemption story?

By God's grace, He has called us His own and taught us . . .

- who He is, through creation, His Word, His Son, and His Spirit;
- His laws of truth, goodness, righteousness, and justice;
- how sin separates us from Him, a holy God;
- how rebelling against God, the source of life, brings death;
- how a pure and perfect blood sacrifice is needed to pay the penalty for sin;
- how Jesus, our substitute sacrifice, has taken our place;
- how Jesus, the Lamb of God who takes away the sins of the world, is our Savior.

Just as Jesus fulfilled every prophecy of His first coming, so Jesus will fulfill every prophecy of His second coming.

God's grand plan was coming, is coming, and will come to pass, from creation to new creation.

What a View!

Our Savior, the Serpent-Slayer, the sacrificial Lamb, the King. He has come, and He is coming again. He will complete the final chapter in this story of all stories. Evil will be eradicated and He shall reign forever.

Those who are found in Christ will thrive once more in God's heavenly kingdom:

- as God's people,
- in God's place,
- under God's leadership and rule.

There, we will enjoy His blessings forever. Sounds like a heavenly vision. And what a view it is!

Given this all-encompassing view, you are now in the best position to comprehend the whole Bible, recognizing how each book points to Christ.

Take heart, my friends! God is not finished yet.

Jesus is the main message of the Bible. He is, and He will take us from creation to new creation. We are headed home!

"For God so loved the world that He gave His only begotten Son, that whoever believes in Him should not perish but have everlasting life" (John 3:16, NKJV).

PART 2

Sixty-Six Readings, Genesis to Revelation

Old Testament Scriptures and Prayers

Day 1—Genesis

God the Creator

In the beginning, God created the heavens and the earth. The earth was without form and void, and darkness was over the face of the deep. And the Spirit of God was hovering over the face of the waters. (Gen. 1:1–2, ESV)

God the Father

Then God said, "Let us make man in our image, after our likeness. And let them have dominion over the fish of the sea and over the birds of the heavens and over the livestock and over all the earth and over every creeping thing that creeps on the earth."

So God created man in his own image,
in the image of God he created him;
male and female he created them.

(1:26–27, ESV)

God the Righteous Lord

Now the serpent was more crafty than any other beast of the field that the Lord God had made. He said to the woman, "Did God actually say, 'You shall not eat of any tree in the garden'?"

And the woman said to the serpent, "We may eat of the fruit of the trees in the garden, but God said, 'You shall not eat of

> the fruit of the tree that is in the midst of the garden, neither shall you touch it, lest you die.'" But the serpent said to the woman, "You will not surely die. For God knows that when you eat of it your eyes will be opened, and you will be like God, knowing good and evil." So when the woman saw that the tree was good for food, and that it was a delight to the eyes, and that the tree was to be desired to make one wise, she took of its fruit and ate, and she also gave some to her husband who was with her, and he ate. (Gen. 3:1–6, ESV)

The serpent tempted Adam and Eve to sin against God; therefore God made this declaration, a foreshadowing of Christ:

> And I will put enmity
> between you and the woman,
> and between your offspring and hers;
> he will crush your head,
> and you will strike his heel.
>
> (3:15, NIV)

The God Who Leads and Blesses

Abraham believed and obeyed God, so God said to him:

> I will surely bless you and make your descendants as numerous as the stars in the sky and as the sand on the seashore. Your descendants will take possession of the cities of their enemies, and through your offspring all nations on earth will be blessed, because you have obeyed me. (22:17–18, NIV)

Prayer

Almighty God, Creator of the heavens and the earth, we praise Your name, for You are unrivaled. You are before all things, above all things, and beyond all things. When we gaze at the height of the heavens, You are higher still. When we ponder the depths of the earth, You are deeper still. For these are merely formed by Your hand, a glimpse of Your fingerprints.

We stand in awe of You. We fear and revere One so powerful. You are God and we are not. Incredibly, You are also our eternal Father. You invite us to draw near, as you did with Adam and Eve in the Garden.

Help us to remember that we are not an accident but a creation of Your hand, made in Your image and precious in Your sight. We thank You, gracious Lord, for You designed us to walk closely with You.

Because of Your absolute goodness, You cannot coexist with evil. You gave mankind holy boundaries, and we chose our sinful way instead. Because of our sin nature, we cannot be in Your perfect Presence unless we are made pure by the blood of Your Son, Jesus Christ.

As believers in Jesus Christ, we no longer need to cover ourselves with the things of this world. By grace through faith, we are now covered by the blood of Jesus and cleansed of our sins.

Help us not to fall prey to the question that still runs rampant: "Did God really say?" Give us a heart to believe Your truth, Your goodness, and Your mercy through Christ Jesus.

Renew our hope with the knowledge that the Garden you planned long ago awaits us just ahead in heaven, where one day we will eat of the Tree of Life.

Thank You, heavenly Father, that through Abraham, You blessed people from every nation to be part of Your kingdom family, as our Savior died for the sins of the whole world. Give us faith like Abraham to follow You.

When we gaze upon the faces of others, help us recognize the image of our Creator in every twinkling eye and cheerful smile. May we run together toward Jesus, rejoicing that all who believe in Christ are born again into Your family! In Jesus' name, Amen.

ꕥ

Day 2—Exodus

The Great I AM

> Then Moses said to God, "If I come to the people of Israel and say to them, 'The God of your fathers has sent me to you,' and they ask me, 'What is his name?' what shall I say to them?" God said to Moses, "I AM WHO I AM." (Exod. 3:13–14, ESV)

The Lord Provides a Sacrificial Lamb

> Then Moses called all the elders of Israel and said to them, "Go and select lambs for yourselves according to your clans, and kill the Passover lamb. Take a bunch of hyssop and dip it in the blood that is in the basin, and touch the lintel and the two doorposts with the blood that is in the basin. None of you shall go out of the door of his house until the morning. For the Lord will pass through to strike the Egyptians, and when he sees the blood on the lintel and on the two doorposts, the Lord will pass over the door and will not allow the destroyer to enter your houses to strike you. You shall observe this rite as a statute for you and for your sons forever. And when you come to the land that the Lord will give you, as he has promised, you shall keep this service. And when your children say to you, 'What do you mean by this service?' you shall say, 'It is the sacrifice of the Lord's Passover, for he passed over the houses of the people of Israel in Egypt, when he struck the Egyptians but spared our houses.'" And the people bowed their heads and worshiped. (12:21–27, ESV)

The Lord Fights for You

God gave Moses these words to speak just before He parted the Red Sea:

> The Lord will fight for you, and you have only to be silent. (14:14, ESV)

The Lord Is Holy (the Ten Commandments)

And God spoke all these words, saying,

"I am the Lord your God, who brought you out of the land of Egypt, out of the house of slavery.

"You shall have no other gods before me.

"You shall not make for yourself a carved image, or any likeness of anything that is in heaven above, or that is in the earth beneath, or that is in the water under the earth. You shall not bow down to them or serve them, for I the Lord your God am a jealous God, visiting the iniquity of the fathers on the children to the third and the fourth generation of those who hate me, but showing steadfast love to thousands of those who love me and keep my commandments.

"You shall not take the name of the Lord your God in vain, for the Lord will not hold him guiltless who takes his name in vain.

"Remember the Sabbath day, to keep it holy. Six days you shall labor, and do all your work, but the seventh day is a Sabbath to the Lord your God. On it you shall not do any work, you, or your son, or your daughter, your male servant, or your female servant, or your livestock, or the sojourner who is within your gates. For in six days the Lord made heaven and earth, the sea, and all that is in them, and rested on the seventh day. Therefore the Lord blessed the Sabbath day and made it holy.

"Honor your father and your mother, that your days may be long in the land that the Lord your God is giving you.

"You shall not murder.

"You shall not commit adultery.

"You shall not steal.

"You shall not bear false witness against your neighbor.

"You shall not covet your neighbor's house; you shall not covet your neighbor's wife, or his male servant, or his female servant, or his ox, or his donkey, or anything that is your neighbor's." (Exod. 20:1–17, ESV)

Prayer

We praise You, Most High God, for You are the great I AM. The One who was, and is, and is to come. You are the unchanging One, the eternal One, the self-existing One, the transcendent One. You are the Sovereign Ruler over all. You are outside of Your creation, and yet You love us enough to enter in and redeem us.

There is no single name to describe the fullness of Your nature. You are our Creator, Father, Provider, Sustainer, Healer, Deliverer, Savior, Master, and King. You are the great I AM!

To oppose the God of life brings death. Thank You for sending Jesus, the sacrificial Lamb of God, to shed His blood on the cross. Then, the wages of sin, namely death, could pass over us. His blood poured down the wooden cross like the lamb's blood dripped on the wooden doorframes of Your people enslaved in Egypt.

When the Egyptians would not relent in their oppression of Your people and opposition to You, You performed miracle after miracle to display Your power. To set Your people free, the oppressors felt the enormity of Your judgment. In Your mercy, You made a way to spare those who follow You.

When the enemy army is behind us, and the Red Sea is before us, we need only rest in You and Your power to save. There is nothing too difficult for You. Your arm is not too short to save. The One who made all things can make all things new. Move in power today, Lord of Hosts! Part the Red Seas in our lives that we may move forward in Your grace and strength.

Almighty God, we bow down before You, for we remember You are holy. You have given us Your laws of righteousness. Your heart is pure, just, righteous, and true. Our souls long for Your goodness, Lord.

Thank You, Jesus. You fulfilled every law of righteousness. Then You laid down Your life as a sacrifice for us, releasing us from the sentence of our unrighteousness.

You are holy, O God. Through Jesus' blood, You have made us holy. Forever, we thank You. In Jesus' name, Amen.

Day 3—Leviticus

God Is Holy, Mankind Is Sinful, a Sacrifice Is Needed

If someone brings a lamb as their sin offering, they are to bring a female without defect. They are to lay their hand on its head and slaughter it for a sin offering at the place where the burnt offering is slaughtered. Then the priest shall take some of the blood of the sin offering with his finger and put it on the horns of the altar of burnt offering and pour out the rest of the blood at the base of the altar. They shall remove all the fat, just as the fat is removed from the lamb of the fellowship offering, and the priest shall burn it on the altar on top of the food offerings presented to the Lord. In this way the priest will make atonement for them for the sin they have committed, and they will be forgiven. (Lev. 4:32–35, NIV)

For I am the Lord your God. Consecrate yourselves therefore, and be holy, for I am holy. (11:44, ESV)

Prayer

Father in heaven, hallowed be Your name. You are holy, separate, pure, and perfect. You are God, and You are good. Because Your goodness is absolute, You cannot allow sin in Your presence.

You are the God of life. We acknowledge that our rebellion and sin bring death. Thank You for providing atonement for our sin by a substitute. A Lamb. A sacrificial Lamb. He lived the life we should have lived and died the death we deserved to die.

O Jesus, Lamb of God, worthy is Your name! Because of You, we are made right with God. Because of You, we are cleansed of our sin. Because of You, we are made presentable before a holy God. Because of You, we are saved. You are our refuge, our covering.

Make us brand new, for we carry Your name.
We thank You.
We worship You.
We love You, Jesus. In Your name, Amen.

Day 4—Numbers

The God Who Dwells with You and Leads You

On the day that the tabernacle was set up, the cloud covered the tabernacle, the tent of the testimony. And at evening it was over the tabernacle like the appearance of fire until morning. So it was always: the cloud covered it by day and the appearance of fire by night. And whenever the cloud lifted from over the tent, after that the people of Israel set out, and in the place where the cloud settled down, there the people of Israel camped. At the command of the Lord the people of Israel set out, and at the command of the Lord they camped. As long as the cloud rested over the tabernacle, they remained in camp. Even when the cloud continued over the tabernacle many days, the people of Israel kept the charge of the Lord and did not set out. Sometimes the cloud was a few days over the tabernacle, and according to the command of the Lord they remained in camp; then according to the command of the Lord they set out. And sometimes the cloud remained from evening until morning. And when the cloud lifted in the morning, they set out, or if it continued for a day and a night, when the cloud lifted they set out. Whether it was two days, or a month, or a longer time, that the cloud continued over the tabernacle, abiding there, the people of Israel remained in camp and did not set out, but when it lifted they set out. At the command of the Lord they camped, and at the command of the Lord they set out. They kept the charge of the Lord, at the command of the Lord by Moses. (Num. 9:15–23, ESV)

The God Who Brings Life From Death

And the staff of the man whom I choose shall sprout. Thus I will make to cease from me the grumblings of the people of Israel, which they grumble against you." Moses spoke to the people of Israel. And all their chiefs gave him staffs, one for each chief, according to their fathers' houses, twelve staffs. And the staff of

Aaron was among their staffs. And Moses deposited the staffs before the Lord in the tent of the testimony.

On the next day Moses went into the tent of the testimony, and behold, the staff of Aaron for the house of Levi had sprouted and put forth buds and produced blossoms, and it bore ripe almonds. Then Moses brought out all the staffs from before the Lord to all the people of Israel. And they looked, and each man took his staff. And the Lord said to Moses, "Put back the staff of Aaron before the testimony, to be kept as a sign for the rebels, that you may make an end of their grumblings against me, lest they die." Thus did Moses; as the Lord commanded him, so he did. (Num. 17:5–11, ESV)

Prayer

We thank You, O Lord, for Your heart of love and leadership. You displayed Your presence among the people as cloud by day and fire by night. May we sense the weight of Your glory in our midst today. May each breath we take remind us of Your breath, Your Spirit, indwelling us and leading us in paths of righteousness for Your name's sake.

Help us look to You. May we go where You go. May we rest when You say, "Rest." Above all, may we seek to abide in Christ, the true Vine, for our soul-nourishment.

You are a good, good Father. May we place our small hands in Your gentle, nail-scarred hands and follow where You lead. Your plans are good.

Heavenly Father, You are the God who upholds us. You are the Giver and Sustainer of life. What once was dead can live again at Your command. Just as Aaron's dead staff sprouted buds, blossomed, and bore ripe almonds overnight, You too can grow new life in our dead and lifeless spirits.

Breathe, Holy Spirit. Breathe new life into us today.
Help us come alive at the sound of your Word,

the move of your Spirit,
and the glory of your Son!

Pulse through these veins with new life, O Lord, and bring forth a harvest of fruitfulness to bless the world around us! In Jesus' name, Amen.

ഗ

Day 5—Deuteronomy

God Gives Strength as We Fear Him and Follow Him

Now this is the commandment—the statutes and the rules—that the Lord your God commanded me to teach you, that you may do them in the land to which you are going over, to possess it, that you may fear the Lord your God, you and your son and your son's son, by keeping all his statutes and his commandments, which I command you, all the days of your life, and that your days may be long. Hear therefore, O Israel, and be careful to do them, that it may go well with you, and that you may multiply greatly, as the Lord, the God of your fathers, has promised you, in a land flowing with milk and honey.

Hear, O Israel: The Lord our God, the Lord is one. You shall love the Lord your God with all your heart and with all your soul and with all your might. And these words that I command you today shall be on your heart. You shall teach them diligently to your children, and shall talk of them when you sit in your house, and when you walk by the way, and when you lie down, and when you rise. You shall bind them as a sign on your hand, and they shall be as frontlets between your eyes. You shall write them on the doorposts of your house and on your gates. (Deut. 6:1–9, ESV)

God Is Loving and Faithful

For you are a people holy to the Lord your God. The Lord your God has chosen you to be a people for his treasured possession, out of all the peoples who are on the face of the earth. It was not because you were more in number than any other people that the Lord set his love on you and chose you, for you were the fewest of all peoples, but it is because the Lord loves you and is keeping the oath that he swore to your fathers, that the Lord has brought you out with a mighty hand and redeemed you from the house of slavery, from the hand of Pharaoh king of Egypt. Know therefore that the Lord your God is God, the faithful God who keeps covenant and steadfast love with those who love him and keep his commandments, to a thousand generations, and repays to their face those who hate him, by destroying them. He will not be slack with one who hates him. He will repay him to his face. You shall therefore be careful to do the commandment and the statutes and the rules that I command you today. (Deut. 7:6–11, ESV)

Prayer

O Lord, our God, we pray for a rightful respect, awe, and reverent fear of You. You are holy. You are God, and there is no other. You are God; there is none like You.

Give us an undivided heart, O Lord. Help us love You first and foremost.

Holy Spirit, write Your Word upon our very souls. Let even our thoughts, perceptions, and emotions be filtered through the truth and grace of Your Word.

Bind it to our hearts. Weave it into the fabric of our beings. Imprint it on our hands. Paint it on our homes.

May Your Word become our word. May Your heart's desire become our heart's desire. May Your ways become our ways. Fill us afresh, Holy Spirit, that we may speak, think, and act like The Word, Jesus Christ.

Heavenly Father, we are Your treasured possession, a chosen people.

Not because of our goodness, but because of Your goodness.

Not because of our faithfulness, but because of Your faithfulness.

Not because we are so loving, but because You are so loving.

You don't love us because we are lovely. Rather, You have loved us, so we are made lovely.

Thank You, Abba Father, for Your love and faithfulness hold us forever. You sought us out. You paid our ransom. You brought us into Your family. How we love You, O Lord! Because You first loved us! In Jesus' name, Amen.

ര

Day 6—Joshua

God is With You Always

> Be strong and courageous, for you shall cause this people to inherit the land that I swore to their fathers to give them. Only be strong and very courageous, being careful to do according to all the law that Moses my servant commanded you. Do not turn from it to the right hand or to the left, that you may have good success wherever you go. This Book of the Law shall not depart from your mouth, but you shall meditate on it day and night, so that you may be careful to do according to all that is written in it. For then you will make your way prosperous, and then you will have good success. Have I not commanded you? Be strong and courageous. Do not be frightened, and do not be dismayed, for the Lord your God is with you wherever you go. (Josh. 1:6–9, ESV)

God Fulfills Every Promise

Joshua said the following to God's people, the Israelites, as they were settled now in the land God promised to Abraham:

> Now I am about to go the way of all the earth. You know with all your heart and soul that not one of all the good promises the Lord your God gave you has failed. Every promise has been fulfilled; not one has failed. (Josh. 23:14, NIV)

Prayer

Mighty God, when You speak, Your strength rises up within us. May we walk in the power of Your indwelling Spirit today. Keep us steady on Your path, following Your ways, not stepping either to the right or the left, but centered in Christ. Holy Spirit, bring scriptures to our minds as we walk today. Help us remember the truth of Your Word.

Rise up strong in us, Holy Spirit! For we carry the Spirit of our resurrected King Jesus within! May we not be afraid. You go with us. You are within us. You are able, Mighty God!

Lord of all, thank You for Your faithfulness. Your Word is final. Whatever You promised, You will bring to pass. As we remember the ways You fulfilled Your promises to the Israelites, we know that You will fulfill every promise from Your Word today.

In Christ Himself, every promise was "yes," and we say "amen" to the glory of God the Father. In Christ, You upheld Your laws of righteousness. You paid the penalty for sins. You defeated sin, death, and Satan. You will come again as triumphant King! May we be found faithful to Christ to the end! In Jesus' name, Amen.

ഗ

Day 7—Judges

God Sent Judges to Lead the People

And the people of Israel did what was evil in the sight of the Lord and served the Baals. And they abandoned the Lord, the God of their fathers, who had brought them out of the land of Egypt. They went after other gods, from among the gods of the peoples who were around them, and bowed down to them. And they provoked the Lord to anger. They abandoned the Lord and served the Baals and the Ashtaroth. (Judg. 2:11–13, ESV)

Then the Lord raised up judges, who saved them out of the hands of these raiders. Yet they would not listen to their judges but prostituted themselves to other gods and worshiped them. They quickly turned from the ways of their ancestors, who had been obedient to the Lord's commands. (2:16–17, NIV)

Now Deborah, a prophet, the wife of Lappidoth, was leading Israel at that time. She held court under the Palm of Deborah between Ramah and Bethel in the hill country of Ephraim, and the Israelites went up to her to have their disputes decided. She sent for Barak son of Abinoam from Kedesh in Naphtali and said to him, "The Lord, the God of Israel, commands you: 'Go, take with you ten thousand men of Naphtali and Zebulun and lead them up to Mount Tabor. I will lead Sisera, the commander of Jabin's army, with his chariots and his troops to the Kishon River and give him into your hands.'"

Barak said to her, "If you go with me, I will go; but if you don't go with me, I won't go."

"Certainly I will go with you," said Deborah. "But because of the course you are taking, the honor will not be yours, for the Lord will deliver Sisera into the hands of a woman." So Deborah went with Barak to Kedesh. There Barak summoned Zebulun and Naphtali, and ten thousand men went up under his command. Deborah also went up with him. (4:4–10, NIV)

In those days there was no king in Israel. Everyone did what was right in his own eyes. (21:25, ESV)

Prayer

Lord Jesus, we praise you, for you are King, Savior, and Judge. You rule rightly and judge justly. You see all and know all. We cry out for the times we have turned from You. Forgive us, O Lord. We recognize that You reach for us again and again, calling us to return to Your heart and return to Your ways.

Holy Spirit, renew our hearts. Plant seeds of righteousness within us through Your Word. Help us seek the Son-shine of your truth and grace. Water us with your refreshing Word, like the dew of heaven. May we not turn away from Your leadership like many have done in the past. Draw us close. Help us not to wander from You or go our own way. Your way is best. In Jesus' name, Amen.

Day 8—Ruth

God Will Provide

> Now Elimelek, Naomi's husband, died, and she was left with her two sons. They married Moabite women, one named Orpah and the other Ruth. After they had lived there about ten years, both Mahlon and Kilion also died, and Naomi was left without her two sons and her husband.
>
> When Naomi heard in Moab that the Lord had come to the aid of his people by providing food for them, she and her daughters-in-law prepared to return home from there. With her two daughters-in-law she left the place where she had been living and set out on the road that would take them back to the land of Judah.
>
> Then Naomi said to her two daughters-in-law, "Go back, each of you, to your mother's home. May the Lord show you kindness, as you have shown kindness to your dead husbands and to me. May the Lord grant that each of you will find rest in the home of another husband." (Ruth 1:3–9, NIV)

But Ruth replied, "Don't urge me to leave you or to turn back from you. Where you go I will go, and where you stay I will stay. Your people will be my people and your God my God. Where you die I will die, and there I will be buried. May the Lord deal with me, be it ever so severely, if even death separates you and me." When Naomi realized that Ruth was determined to go with her, she stopped urging her.

So the two women went on until they came to Bethlehem. When they arrived in Bethlehem, the whole town was stirred because of them, and the women exclaimed, "Can this be Naomi?"

"Don't call me Naomi," she told them. "Call me Mara, because the Almighty has made my life very bitter. I went away full, but the Lord has brought me back empty. Why call me Naomi? The Lord has afflicted me; the Almighty has brought misfortune upon me." (1:16–21, NIV)

So Boaz took Ruth and she became his wife. When he made love to her, the Lord enabled her to conceive, and she gave birth to a son. The women said to Naomi: "Praise be to the Lord, who this day has not left you without a guardian-redeemer. May he become famous throughout Israel! He will renew your life and sustain you in your old age. For your daughter-in-law, who loves you and who is better to you than seven sons, has given him birth."

Then Naomi took the child in her arms and cared for him. The women living there said, "Naomi has a son!" And they named him Obed. He was the father of Jesse, the father of David. (4:13–17, NIV)

Prayer

Lord Jesus, you are our Redeemer. You are our brother, both fully God and fully man. You paid an immeasurable price to win us back at the cost of Your precious, holy blood. We are redeemed by the blood of the Lamb!

You have brought us out of our spiritual poverty like Ruth was brought out of poverty so long ago. You robe us in your righteousness and love. You seat us in heavenly places as part of Your kingdom family. You are coming again to receive Your church, the Bride of Christ.

What a beautiful picture of Your redeeming love for us! Thank you, Lord Jesus! In Your name, Amen.

ɞ

Day 9—First Samuel

God Will Fight For You

> But the Lord said to Samuel, "Do not look on his appearance or on the height of his stature, because I have rejected him. For the Lord sees not as man sees: man looks on the outward appearance, but the Lord looks on the heart." (1 Sam. 16:7, ESV)

David said this to King Saul regarding Goliath:

> "Your servant has struck down both lions and bears, and this uncircumcised Philistine shall be like one of them, for he has defied the armies of the living God." And David said, "The Lord who delivered me from the paw of the lion and from the paw of the bear will deliver me from the hand of this Philistine." And Saul said to David, "Go, and the Lord be with you!"(17:36–37, ESV)

> Then David said to the Philistine, "You come to me with a sword and with a spear and with a javelin, but I come to you in the name of the Lord of hosts, the God of the armies of Israel, whom you have defied. This day the Lord will deliver you into my hand, and I will strike you down and cut off your head. And I will give the dead bodies of the host of the Philistines this day to the birds of the air and to the wild beasts of the earth, that all the earth may know that there is a God in Israel, and that all this assembly may know that the Lord saves

> not with sword and spear. For the battle is the Lord's, and he will give you into our hand."
>
> When the Philistine arose and came and drew near to meet David, David ran quickly toward the battle line to meet the Philistine. And David put his hand in his bag and took out a stone and slung it and struck the Philistine on his forehead. The stone sank into his forehead, and he fell on his face to the ground.
>
> So David prevailed over the Philistine with a sling and with a stone, and struck the Philistine and killed him. There was no sword in the hand of David. (1 Sam. 17:45–50, ESV)

Prayer

Lord God, when You put forth Your mighty hand of strength, who can stand against You? We praise You, for You protect us from dangers seen and unseen. You defend us against physical, emotional, spiritual, and relational attacks. Satan and all the forces of evil cannot overpower You.

Thank You that all we need is faith in You and Your Word. You alone are God. You go before and behind us, above and below. Though our faith be like a small stone, in the hands of God it can accomplish Your unstoppable purposes.

Renew our faith in You and Your power to save! Help us to remember Your indomitable deeds and stand firm in our faith, just as David when he stood before a giant. Our God will never fail! You will fight for us. We need only trust in You. In Jesus' name, Amen.

ಌ

Day 10—Second Samuel

God Is My Rock

And David spoke to the Lord the words of this song on the day when the Lord delivered him from the hand of all his enemies, and from the hand of Saul. He said,

"The Lord is my rock and my fortress and my deliverer,
  my God, my rock, in whom I take refuge,
my shield, and the horn of my salvation,
  my stronghold and my refuge,
  my savior; you save me from violence.
I call upon the Lord, who is worthy to be praised,
  and I am saved from my enemies."

(2 Sam. 22:1–4, ESV)

Prayer

O Lord, our God, You are the ground beneath our feet. You are the breath in our lungs. You are our lifeline, our Champion, our hope, and our strength.

When we are surrounded on every side by obstacles, enemies, hardships, and trials, as with David, You alone are our shield and refuge. When the ground is shifting sand, you are the Rock—immovable, unchanging, steady.

You are our Savior. Praise Your name, Jesus! You have won for us the greatest battle we will ever face, the battle for our souls. Our eternity rests in You, Lord Jesus, for Your blood has won the victory! Forever!

No matter what our earthly eyes may see, no matter what we face in the day ahead, we are unshakable because we are standing on the Rock of Ages. In Your name, Amen.

Day 11—First Kings

God Is My Rest

Now as Solomon finished offering all this prayer and plea to the Lord, he arose from before the altar of the Lord, where he had knelt with hands outstretched toward heaven. And he stood and blessed all the assembly of Israel with a loud voice, saying, "Blessed be the Lord who has given rest to his people Israel, according to all that he promised. Not one word has failed of all his good promise, which he spoke by Moses his servant. The Lord our God be with us, as he was with our fathers. May he not leave us or forsake us, that he may incline our hearts to him, to walk in all his ways and to keep his commandments, his statutes, and his rules, which he commanded our fathers. Let these words of mine, with which I have pleaded before the Lord, be near to the Lord our God day and night, and may he maintain the cause of his servant and the cause of his people Israel, as each day requires, that all the peoples of the earth may know that the Lord is God; there is no other. Let your heart therefore be wholly true to the Lord our God, walking in his statutes and keeping his commandments, as at this day." (1 Kings 8:54–61, ESV)

God Is Lord of All

And at the time of the offering of the oblation, Elijah the prophet came near and said, "O Lord, God of Abraham, Isaac, and Israel, let it be known this day that you are God in Israel, and that I am your servant, and that I have done all these things at your word. Answer me, O Lord, answer me, that this people may know that you, O Lord, are God, and that you have turned their hearts back." Then the fire of the Lord fell and consumed the burnt offering and the wood and the stones and the dust, and licked up the water that was in the trench. And when all the people saw it, they fell on their faces and said, "The Lord, he is God; the Lord, he is God." (18:36–39, ESV)

Prayer

Our Lord and our God, You alone give rest to Your people. As You did with Solomon and the Israelites, so You provide our souls rest today. You alone fulfill every promise found in Your Word. You alone are faithful and true. As You protected Your people through the ages, we know You will protect us this day.

Protect our minds and our hearts. Draw us closer so we may walk in Your ways and keep Your commands. Let Your Word soak into our innermost beings so we abide in Your mercy and truth. May all the peoples of the earth look upon us and see Christ shining through, that they, too, may know the one true and living God.

We also remember that You are a consuming fire. Burn up the chaff within us, as you did when Elijah called, and Your fire fell from heaven. Remove anything we cling to like an idol. Consume anything that is not of You. We lower ourselves prostrate before You, Holy God, to worship and honor You. Show Your power and strength over all things. Let many see and give You glory. For You alone are Lord. In Jesus' name, Amen.

Day 12—Second Kings

The God of Angel Armies

> When the servant of the man of God got up and went out early the next morning, an army with horses and chariots had surrounded the city. "Oh no, my lord! What shall we do?" the servant asked.
>
> "Don't be afraid," the prophet answered. "Those who are with us are more than those who are with them."

And Elisha prayed, "Open his eyes, Lord, so that he may see." Then the Lord opened the servant's eyes, and he looked and saw the hills full of horses and chariots of fire all around Elisha. (2 Kings 6:15–17, NIV)

King of My Heart

The king gave this order to all the people: "Celebrate the Passover to the Lord your God, as it is written in this Book of the Covenant." Neither in the days of the judges who led Israel nor in the days of the kings of Israel and the kings of Judah had any such Passover been observed. But in the eighteenth year of King Josiah, this Passover was celebrated to the Lord in Jerusalem.

Furthermore, Josiah got rid of the mediums and spiritists, the household gods, the idols and all the other detestable things seen in Judah and Jerusalem. This he did to fulfill the requirements of the law written in the book that Hilkiah the priest had discovered in the temple of the Lord. Neither before nor after Josiah was there a king like him who turned to the Lord as he did—with all his heart and with all his soul and with all his strength, in accordance with all the Law of Moses. (2 Kings 23:21–25, NIV)

Prayer

Mighty God, clarify our spiritual vision like Elisha. May we sense Your movements all around. This world is but a faint shadow of Your glorious kingdom. Grant us keen spiritual eyesight to bear witness to the divine chariots of fire that battle in the heavens for Your people. Help us to walk by faith, not by sight, for You are the God of angel armies!

Purify our hearts. Despite earthly idols worshipped in our culture, help us remain true to You. Let Your Word and Your love shine brighter. Lead us in Your ways. Reveal and correct us when we stray from Your commands. Humble us like King Josiah, who turned back to You with all his heart, soul, and strength. Be our desire, be our pursuit, be our treasured prize, above all else. Be the King of our hearts, O Ruler of all. In Jesus' name. Amen.

Day 13—First Chronicles

Christ Our King Forever

David wanted to build a house, or temple, for the Lord.

> Now when David lived in his house, David said to Nathan the prophet, "Behold, I dwell in a house of cedar, but the ark of the covenant of the Lord is under a tent." (1 Chron. 17:1, ESV)

The Lord responded to David's desire to build a house for Him:

> And I will appoint a place for my people Israel and will plant them, that they may dwell in their own place and be disturbed no more. And violent men shall waste them no more, as formerly, from the time that I appointed judges over my people Israel. And I will subdue all your enemies. Moreover, I declare to you that the Lord will build you a house. When your days are fulfilled to walk with your fathers, I will raise up your offspring after you, one of your own sons, and I will establish his kingdom. He shall build a house for me, and I will establish his throne forever. (17:9–12, ESV)

Prayer

Praise the name of Jesus! Son of God and Son of Man. Righteous One, spotless Lamb, victorious One, King forever! We exalt Your great name, O Lord, for You declared long ago that which You would bring to pass. Jesus Christ, born in Bethlehem, of the line of David. Jesus Christ fulfilled every prophecy that was foretold. You established the throne of David through our everlasting King, Jesus Christ.

Likewise, every prophecy of Jesus' second coming will be fulfilled, for the mouth of the Lord has spoken. We rest assured that one day, You will make a new heaven and a new earth, and the dwelling place of God will be with mankind. There, we will worship Christ, our triumphant Savior and glorious King forever. THE KING OF KINGS AND LORD OF LORDS!

In Jesus' mighty name. Amen.

Day 14—Second Chronicles

The God Who Forgives

> Thus Solomon finished the house of the Lord and the king's house. All that Solomon had planned to do in the house of the Lord and in his own house he successfully accomplished. Then the Lord appeared to Solomon in the night and said to him: "I have heard your prayer and have chosen this place for myself as a house of sacrifice. When I shut up the heavens so that there is no rain, or command the locust to devour the land, or send pestilence among my people, if my people who are called by my name humble themselves, and pray and seek my face and turn from their wicked ways, then I will hear from heaven and will forgive their sin and heal their land. Now my eyes will be open and my ears attentive to the prayer that is made in this place. For now I have chosen and consecrated this house that my name may be there forever. My eyes and my heart will be there for all time." (2 Chron. 7:11–16, ESV)

Prayer

Holy Spirit, You have made Your dwelling place within our hearts. Such a sacred and precious gift we bear! Enlarge our hearts and minds to take in the fullness of this heaven-sent treasure we carry about in these frail vessels of clay. As we embody the Spirit of Christ within, Your eyes and Your heart indwell our very being.

As you taught Solomon, help us to humble ourselves and turn from any wicked ways. We seek Your face. Expose any secret sins or hidden faults we cannot see. We desire to be holy as You are holy. Remove all pride, arrogance, and self-reliance.

Give us surrendered hearts and teachable spirits, willing to be shaped by the Potter's hands. As we set down our pride, there is more space for You in the home of our hearts. Move in, Lord Jesus. Fill every room, corner, crack, and crevice with Your overflowing light and love. We consecrate every part of ourselves to You. In Jesus' name, Amen.

Day 15—Ezra

God Accomplishes His Purposes

> So the elders of the Jews continued to build and prosper under the preaching of Haggai the prophet and Zechariah, a descendant of Iddo. They finished building the temple according to the command of the God of Israel and the decrees of Cyrus, Darius and Artaxerxes, kings of Persia. The temple was completed on the third day of the month Adar, in the sixth year of the reign of King Darius. Then the people of Israel—the priests, the Levites and the rest of the exiles—celebrated the dedication of the house of God with joy. (Ezra 6:14–16, NIV)

Prayer

Great are You, Lord! You hold all things in Your hands. You hold all time in Your hands. You hold all people in Your hands. You accomplish Your purposes in our lives and throughout eternity. You bring forth Your immutable plans.

How great are You, Lord! Your timetable is irrepressible. If it is Your will, it will come to pass. May we rest in Your unfailing power, Your enduring good, and Your unchanging Word. We remember the Israelites who dedicated the newly rebuilt temple, so we dedicate ourselves to You. We are the temple of Your Holy Spirit. Help us to sense Your presence and glory. May the joy of the Lord surge from within to bless the world. In Jesus' name, Amen.

Day 16—Nehemiah

God Hears Our Prayers of Repentance

The words of Nehemiah son of Hakaliah:

In the month of Kislev in the twentieth year, while I was in the citadel of Susa, Hanani, one of my brothers, came from Judah with some other men, and I questioned them about the Jewish remnant that had survived the exile, and also about Jerusalem.

They said to me, "Those who survived the exile and are back in the province are in great trouble and disgrace. The wall of Jerusalem is broken down, and its gates have been burned with fire."

When I heard these things, I sat down and wept. For some days I mourned and fasted and prayed before the God of heaven. Then I said:

"Lord, the God of heaven, the great and awesome God, who keeps his covenant of love with those who love him and keep his commandments, let your ear be attentive and your eyes open to hear the prayer your servant is praying before you day and night for your servants, the people of Israel. I confess the sins we Israelites, including myself and my father's family, have committed against you. We have acted very wickedly toward you. We have not obeyed the commands, decrees and laws you gave your servant Moses.

"Remember the instruction you gave your servant Moses, saying, 'If you are unfaithful, I will scatter you among the nations, but if you return to me and obey my commands, then even if your exiled people are at the farthest horizon, I will gather them from there and bring them to the place I have chosen as a dwelling for my Name.'

"They are your servants and your people, whom you redeemed by your great strength and your mighty hand. Lord, let your ear be attentive to the prayer of this your servant and to the

> prayer of your servants who delight in revering your name. Give your servant success today by granting him favor in the presence of this man."

I was cupbearer to the king. (Neh. 1:1–11 NIV)

Prayer

Lord, God of heaven, we join with Your people through the ages to declare that You are an awesome God. As great as You are, so great is Your love for us. Lord Jesus, You pour out Your love upon Your people, those whose hearts are for You and who keep Your commands.

Thank You, O God, for Your steadfast love and faithfulness. Thank You, O God, for Your heart of forgiveness. When we have gone astray from Your path of righteousness, if we repent and turn back to You, You take us back into your fold. Like the father who opened his arms to the prodigal son, so You open wide Your nail-scarred hands for any sinner who will turn from sin and run to You.

Holy Spirit, search our hearts. As in the days of Nehemiah, when your people returned to You, You brought them home and bestowed Your favor upon them. Help us be honest with ourselves and with You about our sin. Show us the way of escape from each sin. Ignite our hearts with a fresh desire to step away from our sinful muck and leap into Your arms of healing, truth, forgiveness, purity, and love. In Jesus' name, Amen.

ಌ

Day 17—Esther

God Saves His People

> When Esther's words were reported to Mordecai, he sent back this answer: "Do not think that because you are in the king's house you alone of all the Jews will escape. For if you remain silent at this time, relief and deliverance for the Jews will arise from another place, but you and your father's family will perish. And who knows but that you have come to your royal position for such a time as this?"
>
> Then Esther sent this reply to Mordecai: "Go, gather together all the Jews who are in Susa, and fast for me. Do not eat or drink for three days, night or day. I and my attendants will fast as you do. When this is done, I will go to the king, even though it is against the law. And if I perish, I perish." (Esther 4:12–16, NIV)

Prayer

Holy God, You rule and reign. You place people into positions. You orchestrate every detail. Though Satan's goals are to steal, kill, and destroy, when we cry out for Your protection, we are safe and secure in Christ.

Spirit of God, breathe into us fresh courage to rise up, like Esther, to stand strong in You. Help us observe Your commands and be an example for Your people, come what may. May we never depart from Your Word to the left or to the right. Move the mountains before us. Help us to walk in safety and proclaim to all, "Our God reigns!"

Thank You, Lord Jesus, for You have already gone to the cross and back to save Your people. For all who confess You as Savior and Lord, the greatest battle is done. May we hold tight to Your hand, knowing whatever battle we face, our fiercest enemy, Satan, is already defeated. Help us walk in the victory that You won for us on the cross. With God, nothing is impossible! In Jesus' all-powerful name, Amen.

Day 18—Job

My Redeemer Lives

One day when Job's sons and daughters were feasting and drinking wine at the oldest brother's house, a messenger came to Job and said, "The oxen were plowing and the donkeys were grazing nearby, and the Sabeans attacked and made off with them. They put the servants to the sword, and I am the only one who has escaped to tell you!"

While he was still speaking, another messenger came and said, "The fire of God fell from the heavens and burned up the sheep and the servants, and I am the only one who has escaped to tell you!"

While he was still speaking, another messenger came and said, "The Chaldeans formed three raiding parties and swept down on your camels and made off with them. They put the servants to the sword, and I am the only one who has escaped to tell you!"

While he was still speaking, yet another messenger came and said, "Your sons and daughters were feasting and drinking wine at the oldest brother's house, when suddenly a mighty wind swept in from the desert and struck the four corners of the house. It collapsed on them and they are dead, and I am the only one who has escaped to tell you!"

At this, Job got up and tore his robe and shaved his head. Then he fell to the ground in worship and said:

> "Naked I came from my mother's womb,
> and naked I will depart.
> The Lord gave and the Lord has taken away;
> may the name of the Lord be praised."

In all this, Job did not sin by charging God with wrongdoing. (Job 1:13–22, NIV)

For I know that my Redeemer lives,
  and at the last he will stand upon the earth.
And after my skin has been thus destroyed,
  yet in my flesh I shall see God,
whom I shall see for myself,
  and my eyes shall behold, and not another.
  My heart faints within me!

(Job 19:25–27, ESV)

Prayer

Almighty God, you are sovereign Ruler. Your ways are higher than our ways. Your thoughts are higher than ours. We know that above all, You are good. When you permit heartache and difficulties to befall us, we know You are still God, and You are still good. Grant us faith like Job to trust you even in the valleys.

As stormy seasons force us to lean into You, we remember the gift of Your presence is a priceless treasure. Through bleakest moments, You orchestrate situations to bring forth Your shining glory and our ultimate good.

We thank You, Lord, for on the day Jesus died on the cross, what seemed to be the worst possible evil of all time became the best possible good of all time. In Your hands all things worked together for good. The One who died for our sins, rose again! Our Redeemer lives! Because He lives, we live, too! Oh what a Savior! In Jesus' precious name, Amen.

ᔓ

Day 19—Psalms

The God Who Sees Me

You have searched me, Lord,
  and you know me.
You know when I sit and when I rise;
  you perceive my thoughts from afar.
You discern my going out and my lying down;
  you are familiar with all my ways.
Before a word is on my tongue
  you, Lord, know it completely.
You hem me in behind and before,
  and you lay your hand upon me.
Such knowledge is too wonderful for me,
  too lofty for me to attain.

Where can I go from your Spirit?
  Where can I flee from your presence?
If I go up to the heavens, you are there;
  if I make my bed in the depths, you are there.
If I rise on the wings of the dawn,
  if I settle on the far side of the sea,
even there your hand will guide me,
  your right hand will hold me fast.
If I say, "Surely the darkness will hide me
  and the light become night around me,"
even the darkness will not be dark to you;
  the night will shine like the day,
  for darkness is as light to you.

For you created my inmost being;
  you knit me together in my mother's womb.
I praise you because I am fearfully and wonderfully made;
  your works are wonderful,
  I know that full well.
My frame was not hidden from you
  when I was made in the secret place,
  when I was woven together in the depths of the earth.

Your eyes saw my unformed body;
all the days ordained for me were written in your book
before one of them came to be. . . .

Search me, God, and know my heart;
test me and know my anxious thoughts.
See if there is any offensive way in me,
and lead me in the way everlasting.

(Ps. 139:1–7, 23–24, NIV)

Prayer

Heavenly Father, how amazing You are! You aligned the planets one by one. You hung the stars in place and called them by name. With a mighty hand and outstretched arm You paint each sunrise with the artistry of heaven. Your vastness is beyond fathoming. Yet, You formed me in my mother's womb, and You call me by name. You know me inside and out. You count every hair on my head!

You made me. You know me. You love me, more than anyone else ever could.

Incredibly, through Jesus, You gave me something even more. You called me to be born again. Not born of flesh and blood, but born of Your Holy Spirit.

Now we are sons and daughters of the Most High God. Not merely part of Your creation, but part of Your eternal family!

Make me brand new in Christ. Help me taste anew Your immeasurable love for me. Help me breathe in Your divine wisdom. Help me grasp onto Your steady hands wounded with mercy for me. Help me walk in Your footsteps of truth, exuding the fragrance of heaven and speaking the mercies of Your Word wherever You may lead.

Search through me from head to toe. Shine your beaming flashlight of truth into the dingy, dark corners of my being. Sweep away sin, and polish the jagged edges of my heart. Let me reflect the unending light of Christ. In His name, Amen.

Day 20—Proverbs

God of Wisdom

Trust in the Lord with all your heart
  and lean not on your own understanding;
in all your ways submit to him,
  and he will make your paths straight.

Do not be wise in your own eyes;
  fear the Lord and shun evil.

(Prov. 3:5–7, NIV)

Who has gone up to heaven and come down?
  Whose hands have gathered up the wind?
Who has wrapped up the waters in a cloak?
  Who has established all the ends of the earth?
What is his name, and what is the name of his son?
  Surely you know!

Every word of God is flawless;
  he is a shield to those who take refuge in him.
Do not add to his words,
  or he will rebuke you and prove you a liar.

(30:4–6, NIV)

Prayer

Most High God, You are Creator of the heavens and earth. There is none like You. With Your voice the universe took its shape. Every molecule is held in place by Your command. Great are You, Lord.

We praise You, Jesus, for You are the Word from the beginning. The triune God: God the Father, God the Son, God the Spirit.

Holy Spirit, give us a rightful fear, awe, and reverence of Your majesty and the weight of Your holiness. We bow low in Your Presence for we are standing on holy ground. Grow in us a wholehearted trust in You, our Maker.

Help us to seek wisdom—not earthly wisdom, but Your wisdom from above. Help us to recognize our finite life before One so great.

Your Words will stand forever, while the words of mankind float away at day's end. Help us trust You, lean on Your Word, and follow You in all our ways. Help us to anchor ourselves in You and You alone. In Jesus' name, Amen.

ꕥ

Day 21—Ecclesiastes

God Is Our Just Judge

Now all has been heard;
   here is the conclusion of the matter:
Fear God and keep his commandments,
   for this is the duty of all mankind.
For God will bring every deed into judgment,
   including every hidden thing,
   whether it is good or evil.

(Eccles. 12:13–14 NIV)

Prayer

Mighty God, like a small child before a Supreme Court Judge, even more so are we before You, the Ruler and Judge of all. You see all, and You know all. Your justice and righteousness are absolute and perfect, for You look upon the heart.

At the end of our days, we will give an account to You for the things we have done.

We thank You for the cross, O Jesus. The one place where justice, love, and forgiveness defeat evil.

Every sin of mankind was laid upon Your shoulders, thus upholding God's righteousness and justice. You paid the penalty due for our sins in the courtroom of heaven. And now we are clothed in Your righteousness instead.

Justice paid. Then mercy given.

Give us a heart of humble appreciation. Help us keep Your commandments, for Your ways are right, just, and true. May we live to please You from a heart of overflowing gratitude. In Jesus' name, Amen.

ꕤ

Day 22—Song of Solomon

God Is Love

Place me like a seal over your heart,
  like a seal on your arm;
for love is as strong as death,
  its jealousy unyielding as the grave.
It burns like blazing fire,
  like a mighty flame. (Song 8:6, NIV)

Prayer

God, You are love. All pure love springs from You and displays Your likeness. Like the love of a devoted husband for his beloved wife, so is Your love, O Jesus, for Your church.

May Your unfailing, sacrificial love enfold me, cover me and warm me. Captivate my heart anew. May the flames of love burn bright within me, ignited by Your holy love for Your church, the Bride of Christ.

You have written me on the palms of Your hands. You have sealed me with Your Holy Spirit. Your love for me is complete, steady, all-consuming. Stir in my heart a devoted love response. For no one loves me more than You. In Your name, Amen.

ꕤ

Day 23—Isaiah

God's Sacrificial Love

But he was pierced for our transgressions,
he was crushed for our iniquities;
the punishment that brought us peace was on him,
and by his wounds we are healed.
We all, like sheep, have gone astray,
each of us has turned to our own way;
and the Lord has laid on him
the iniquity of us all.

(Isa. 53:5–6, NIV)

Prayer

Jesus, O Jesus, we cannot fathom such love. Recorded in Isaiah, prophesied long before You walked on this earth, Your sacrifice of love is foretold.

You poured out Your love in rivers of blood on Calvary's cross. You settled our sin-debt in heaven. By Your wounds, my sin-sick soul is healed forever. Immeasurable, incredible, sacrificial love of God.

How You loved the whole world! How You gave of Yourself to the end! You are the Christ, the Savior, the Messiah. The Great Shepherd turned and became the Lamb of God. Amazing grace. Amazing mercy. Amazing love.

Thank You for such a gift of love. Eternity will not be long enough to thank You, Jesus.

In Your name, Amen.

Day 24—Jeremiah

God of Our Future

> "For I know the plans I have for you," declares the Lord, "plans to prosper you and not to harm you, plans to give you hope and a future. Then you will call on me and come and pray to me, and I will listen to you. You will seek me and find me when you seek me with all your heart." (Jer. 29:11–13, NIV)

Prayer

Eternal God, You know the end from the beginning. And what a glorious end You have prepared for us! Eternal rest, eternal peace, eternal joy in Your presence, where there will be no more tears or sorrow or pain.

We see the depths of Your goodness when we look into the face of Christ. Your desire is that no one would perish, but that all would come to a saving knowledge of the truth: Jesus Christ saves. So, we know Your plans for us are good. Because of Jesus, we have unshakable hope and a future of infinite beauty.

Thank you, Gracious Father, for moving mountains of sin, parting seas of doubt, stilling the stormy waves of our hearts, as we walk in faith ever closer with You, day by day. Let our prayers to You ring out in the heavens. Give us an unquenchable thirst for the Living Water of Your presence. Help us to seek You more and more, for our souls rest only when we rest in You.

In Jesus' name, Amen.

Day 25—Lamentations

God Is Faithful

I remember my affliction and my wandering,
the bitterness and the gall.
I well remember them,
and my soul is downcast within me.
Yet this I call to mind
and therefore I have hope:

Because of the Lord's great love we are not consumed,
for his compassions never fail.
They are new every morning;
great is your faithfulness.
I say to myself, "The Lord is my portion;
therefore I will wait for him."

(Lam. 3:19–24, NIV)

Prayer

Gracious God, when I look back through my failures and wayward steps, I see how You gently whispered my name. You opened doors of blessing and closed doors of self-centeredness to lead me back to You.

During difficult days, Your steadfast love and unending mercy gave me hope.

How many times have You forgiven me? How many times have You led me back home?

Great is your faithfulness, O God, my Father. Though I stumble and falter, as soon as I repent and return to You, Your mercy greets me with tender song.

Spirit of God, lead my steps today. For Your mercies are new every morning, as certain as the dawn of a new day. You are my source, my strength, my breath, my life, my hope. You are my portion.

Thank You, my faithful Father. In Jesus' name, Amen.

☙

Day 26—Ezekiel

God Gives Me a New Heart

I will give you a new heart and put a new spirit in you; I will remove from you your heart of stone and give you a heart of flesh. And I will put my Spirit in you and move you to follow my decrees and be careful to keep my laws. Then you will live in the land I gave your ancestors; you will be my people, and I will be your God. (Ezek. 36:26–28, NIV)

Prayer

Creator God, create in me a new heart. A soft heart, that radiates the warmth and love of Christ. Cut away any hardness, places where past hurts and failures have deadened me.

Resuscitate me, O Lord, with Your breath of life. Do open-heart surgery to heal me from any cancer of pride or self-exaltation. Let Your Spirit set the beat of my heart to the rhythm of Yours. May the heartbeat of heaven be my song.

Write Your laws on my heart. Let me see the beauty, goodness, and purity of every Word You have spoken. May I long to walk in step with You. For I am Yours and You are mine. My God, my Savior, my Lord. In Jesus' name, Amen.

Day 27—Daniel

God Gives Wisdom

> The king replied to the astrologers, "This is what I have firmly decided: If you do not tell me what my dream was and interpret it, I will have you cut into pieces and your houses turned into piles of rubble. But if you tell me the dream and explain it, you will receive from me gifts and rewards and great honor. So tell me the dream and interpret it for me." (Dan. 2:5–6, NIV)

> During the night the mystery was revealed to Daniel in a vision. Then Daniel praised the God of heaven and said:
>
> "Praise be to the name of God for ever and ever;
> wisdom and power are his.
> He changes times and seasons;
> he deposes kings and raises up others.
> He gives wisdom to the wise
> and knowledge to the discerning.
> He reveals deep and hidden things;
> he knows what lies in darkness,
> and light dwells with him.
> I thank and praise you, God of my ancestors:
> You have given me wisdom and power,
> you have made known to me what we asked of you,
> you have made known to us the dream of the king."
>
> (Dan. 2:19–23, NIV)

God Protects

Daniel's fellow administrators were jealous of him, so they tried to trap him by persuading the king to issue the following decree: anyone who prayed to any man or god except King Darius for the next thirty days would be thrown into the lion's den (6:6–9). Daniel, however, refused to stop praying to God.

So the king gave the order, and they brought Daniel and threw him into the lions' den. The king said to Daniel, "May your God, whom you serve continually, rescue you!" . . .

At the first light of dawn, the king got up and hurried to the lions' den. When he came near the den, he called to Daniel in an anguished voice, "Daniel, servant of the living God, has your God, whom you serve continually, been able to rescue you from the lions?"

Daniel answered, "May the king live forever! My God sent his angel, and he shut the mouths of the lions. They have not hurt me, because I was found innocent in his sight. Nor have I ever done any wrong before you, Your Majesty." (Dan. 6:16, 19–22, NIV)

Prayer

Lord God of Hosts, You are omnipotent. Creator and Master over all. You reveal wisdom, knowledge, and discernment of hidden things. All-seeing, all-knowing, all-powerful, ever-present, Most High God. Your foresight and understanding are unparalleled.

As believers in Jesus, we have the mind of Christ. We invite You, Holy Spirit, to teach us Your wisdom and Your Word. Show us the deep beauty and wonderful mysteries that are beyond us. Let us gaze upon Your glory as we mine the depths of Your truth.

We praise You for Your sovereign strength and unrivaled protection. As You did with Daniel, You shut the mouths of lions to keep us safe. You walk with us in the fire. When we are surrounded and attacked by Satan, the enemy of our soul, we call to Jesus and we are saved. There is power in Your name, Jesus! In Your name we pray, Amen.

Day 28—Hosea

Jesus Christ Saves

There I will give her back her vineyards,
  and will make the Valley of Achor [trouble] a door of hope.
There she will respond as in the days of her youth,
  as in the day she came up out of Egypt. (Hos. 2:15, NIV)

I will plant her for myself in the land;
  I will show my love to the one I called 'Not my loved one.'
I will say to those called 'Not my people,' 'You are my people';
  and they will say, 'You are my God.'" (2:23, NIV)

"Come, let us return to the Lord.
He has torn us to pieces
  but he will heal us;
he has injured us
  but he will bind up our wounds.
After two days he will revive us;
  on the third day he will restore us,
  that we may live in his presence.
Let us acknowledge the Lord;
  let us press on to acknowledge him.
As surely as the sun rises,
  he will appear;
he will come to us like the winter rains,
  like the spring rains that water the earth." (6:1–3, NIV)

Prayer

Lord Jesus, You are the doorway to heaven, the gateway to a right relationship with the Father. A heavenly communion. A holy bond. You are our door of hope.

We brought You our dirt, impurity, sin, and rebellion. You lifted our sin-laden souls and healed us at the cross. Our hearts were torn to pieces, but by Your stripes we are healed. You are a divine balm. A soul-healer. Because of Your sacrifice, we are called by Your name, we are Your people, beloved children of God.

Give us a heart to know You, to love You, to press on to acknowledge who You are and who we are in You.

As surely as morning sun warms our face, so your Son-light will shine when You come again ablaze in triumphant glory. Help us to open wide the gates of our hearts to welcome in the King of glory! In Your name, Amen.

❧

Day 29—Joel

God's Spirit Is Poured Out

And afterward,
I will pour out my Spirit on all people.
Your sons and daughters will prophesy,
your old men will dream dreams,
your young men will see visions.
Even on my servants, both men and women,
I will pour out my Spirit in those days.
I will show wonders in the heavens
and on the earth,
blood and fire and billows of smoke.
The sun will be turned to darkness
and the moon to blood
before the coming of the great and dreadful day of the Lord.
And everyone who calls
on the name of the Lord will be saved.

(Joel 2:28–32, NIV)

Prayer

Lord God, You are Spirit, and all who worship You must worship in spirit and in truth. Pour out Your Spirit upon Your people, those who have claimed Christ as Savior and LORD.

Revive us. Renew us. Refresh us. Remake us. Open our eyes to see Your wonders above and below. Give us Your fiery vision to burn within, blazing truth and consuming devotion.

Move in power, Holy Spirit. Move the mountains that block our work for Your kingdom. Breathe new life into our dry bones. Make us alive again with the Living Water of Christ that flows through our veins.

Speak Your Word into our dreams. Help us partner with You to bring about Your kingdom purposes before that day when You come again. Help us to share the good news, rejoicing that all who call on the name of the Lord will be saved.

Help us to be a beacon of Christ's light for all to see, an intercom system for all to hear that Jesus saves! Holy Spirit, let the lost hear Jesus knocking on the door of their hearts. Let them receive Christ, for He will come and save. He is God, and there is no other! Let them call out His name and find new life in Christ! In His name, Amen.

Day 30—Amos

God Restores

This is what the Lord says:

"For three sins of Judah,
even for four, I will not relent.
Because they have rejected the law of the Lord
and have not kept his decrees,
because they have been led astray by false gods,
the gods their ancestors followed.

(Amos 2:4, NIV)

But let justice roll on like a river,
righteousness like a never-failing stream!

(5:24, NIV)

"The days are coming," declares the Lord,

"when the reaper will be overtaken by the plowman
  and the planter by the one treading grapes.
New wine will drip from the mountains
  and flow from all the hills,
  and I will bring my people Israel back from exile.

"They will rebuild the ruined cities and live in them.
  They will plant vineyards and drink their wine;
  they will make gardens and eat their fruit.
I will plant Israel in their own land,
  never again to be uprooted
  from the land I have given them,"

says the Lord your God.

(9:13–15, NIV)

Prayer

Holy God, forgive us. How easily we fall into Satan's traps, rejecting Your laws, compromising Your commands, following the world's philosophies and ideologies, putting people and things ahead of You, making them our idols.

How quickly we forget Your goodness. How quickly we run to lesser things, counterfeit versions of real truth and love. How quickly we substitute anything for You. Forgive us, O Lord.

May the justice of heaven roll down over us, refreshing and resetting our minds on Your Word. May the righteousness that Christ won for us on the cross renew our desire to become like Him—holy, pure, and merciful.

Thank You, heavenly Father, that You have spoken. Restoration has begun. Restoration is happening. Complete restoration will be done.

For Christ has rebuilt our broken lives with His blood shed on Calvary. Christ is reshaping us into His image day by day, growing us in the wisdom and ways of God. Christ will rule and reign forever when He returns once again, and our final restoration is complete.

May we walk side by side with You, building Your kingdom stone upon stone—a living temple of stones built on Christ, our Cornerstone; Christ, the Restorer of the nations; Christ, the Restorer of me. In His name, Amen.

ꕥ

Day 31—Obadiah

God Is Judge of the Nations

The pride of your heart has deceived you,
you who live in the clefts of the rocks
and make your home on the heights,
you who say to yourself,
'Who can bring me down to the ground?'
(Obad. 1:3, NIV)

The day of the Lord
is near for all nations.
As you have done, it will be done to you;
your deeds will return upon your own head.
(1:15, NIV)

Christ Is Our Deliverer

But on Mount Zion will be deliverance;
it will be holy,
and Jacob will possess his inheritance.
(1:17, NIV)

Prayer

Almighty God, You are high and lifted up. You are Creator God and Lord over all. May pride not overtake us. May arrogance not rise up within us. Help us to see Christ, Savior of the world, hanging on the cross for our sins—the mighty One, the Champion, the Deliverer.

The Word from the beginning spoke His mercy over us that day. May pride lose its hold as we gaze into the eyes of our suffering Savior, our merciful King, our sacrificial Shepherd. May humility seep into our frame as we remember Him. The One who made the trees hung on a tree so we could feast on the Tree of Life in heaven forever. Let humility lead us. Help us to decrease, so Christ can increase.

For one Day soon, all will give an account before our Maker—every nation, every tribe, every person.

But for Jesus, we would have no hope. But for Jesus, we would stand condemned, guilty as charged. Glory to God, our Deliverer has come! We have been set free. Jesus has won for us an eternal inheritance. We are adopted into the family of God. The Judge took our place, received our sentence, and we are free! Our Deliver has come and is coming again! In Jesus' name, Amen.

Day 32—Jonah

God Sees All

> The word of the Lord came to Jonah son of Amittai: "Go to the great city of Nineveh and preach against it, because its wickedness has come up before me."
>
> But Jonah ran away from the Lord and headed for Tarshish. He went down to Joppa, where he found a ship bound for that port. After paying the fare, he went aboard and sailed for Tarshish to flee from the Lord. (Jon. 1:1–3, NIV)
>
> Then they took Jonah and threw him overboard, and the raging sea grew calm. (1:15, NIV)
>
> Now the Lord provided a huge fish to swallow Jonah, and Jonah was in the belly of the fish three days and three nights. (1:17, NIV)

> From inside the fish Jonah prayed to the Lord his God. He said:
>
> "In my distress I called to the Lord,
> and he answered me.
> From deep in the realm of the dead I called for help,
> and you listened to my cry. . . .
>
> And the Lord commanded the fish, and it vomited Jonah onto dry land. (2:1–2, 10, NIV)

God Forgives When We Repent

> When God saw what they did and how they [the people of Nineveh] turned from their evil ways, he relented and did not bring on them the destruction he had threatened. (3:10, NIV)

Jonah was angry about this, but the Lord said to him,

> "And should I not have concern for the great city of Nineveh, in which there are more than a hundred and twenty thousand people who cannot tell their right hand from their left—and also many animals?" (Jonah 4:11, NIV)

Prayer

Mighty God, You are omniscient. You know all, You see all, and You respond with a heart of truth and mercy.

You are omnipotent. You have all power to carry out Your will and advance Your holy purposes in heaven and on earth. One glance of Your eyes, one breath from Your mouth, and it is done.

You are omnipresent. Though You exist outside of Your creation, there is nowhere in the expansive universe that You are not there. For the universe itself is but the work of Your hands. You are so far beyond us.

You see our sin. You see our rebellion. You see our defiance. You see our desire to go our own way. As we think of Jonah, Lord God, help us bear in mind wherever we are, You can see.

You can see when we speak in tenderness to those who are hurting. You can see when we stare in anger at those who have hurt us. You are with us always. Speaking, leading, calling us to live like Jesus.

Give us repentant hearts, soft as clay in Your Potter's hands—willing to be corrected, willing to be disciplined, willing to be changed into the image of our precious Savior.

Help us forgive others, as You have forgiven us. Redesign our hearts to reflect Yours. A heart of truth regarding our own sin. Please give us heart of forgiveness for others. In Jesus' name, Amen.

ᔕ

Day 33—Micah

God of Justice, Mercy, and Humility

With what shall I come before the Lord
  and bow down before the exalted God?
Shall I come before him with burnt offerings,
  with calves a year old?
Will the Lord be pleased with thousands of rams,
  with ten thousand rivers of olive oil?
Shall I offer my firstborn for my transgression,
  the fruit of my body for the sin of my soul?
He has shown you, O mortal, what is good.
  And what does the Lord require of you?
To act justly and to love mercy
  and to walk humbly with your God.

(Mic. 6:6–8, NIV)

Prayer

Almighty God, creation belongs to You. The heavens are Yours, the seas, also. The mountains, the hills, the valleys, the rivers and streams, every creature great and small, they belong to You. You own the cattle on a thousand hills.

With what shall we come before You, O Lord, to bow down before the exalted God? What offering could we bring to atone for our sins?

There is one—only one. Faith in Christ alone. He is our justice. He is our righteousness. He is our mercy. Jesus, our humble Savior, leads us.

Let me walk hand in hand with Christ, living out His justice, loving others with His mercy, walking humbly with God all my days. In Jesus' name, Amen.

ꟹ

Day 34—Nahum

God Judges and Destroys Evil

The Lord is slow to anger but great in power;
the Lord will not leave the guilty unpunished.
His way is in the whirlwind and the storm,
and clouds are the dust of his feet.
He rebukes the sea and dries it up;
he makes all the rivers run dry.
Bashan and Carmel wither
and the blossoms of Lebanon fade.
The mountains quake before him
and the hills melt away.
The earth trembles at his presence,
the world and all who live in it.
Who can withstand his indignation?
Who can endure his fierce anger?

(Nah. 1:3–6, NIV)

Whatever they plot against the Lord
he will bring to an end;
trouble will not come a second time.

(1:9, NIV)

Prayer

Gracious God, thank You for Your steadfast love and faithfulness. You are slow to anger. Yet You do not allow evil to go unchecked. Every sin is accounted for.

We are either forgiven in Christ, or we stand condemned before You. The earth itself trembles at Your sovereignty and fierce power. Who can stand against You?

You are a forgiving God when we repent and seek Your face.

But still . . . You are God. You are holy. You will not be mocked.

May those who continue to do evil be exposed. May every evil carried out against children, against the elderly, against the vulnerable, be brought to light.

First, Lord, we pray for repentance, for sins we have committed and for others who have committed sins against us. Yet, for any who are unwilling to follow Your commands of righteousness, who are carrying out evil plans against us, we rest in your justice.

You have said, "Vengeance is mine. I will repay."

Help us to not take things into our own hands. Help us to trust in Your absolute justice, which will be executed through Christ. Satan and all evil will be accounted for on Judgment Day. We abide in Your truth, Your holiness, and Your mercy in Christ. The battle belongs to You. In Jesus' name, Amen.

ൾ

Day 35—Habakkuk

The Lord Is Our Strength

Though the fig tree does not bud
and there are no grapes on the vines,
though the olive crop fails
and the fields produce no food,
though there are no sheep in the pen
and no cattle in the stalls,
yet I will rejoice in the Lord,
I will be joyful in God my Savior.
The Sovereign Lord is my strength;
he makes my feet like the feet of a deer,
he enables me to tread on the heights.
(Hab. 3:17–19, NIV)

Prayer

Sovereign Lord, You are my strength. You lift my spirit. You encourage my heart. You anchor my mind. You secure my body. You are my strength and my shield, my fortress in the time of storms.

When all else has failed me. When there seems nothing left. I call to mind that You alone are my source.

Everything I have comes from You. Food, water, family, education, job opportunities, gifts, and talents. You are the source of life, health, and strength. When I have nothing else in this world, I still have You and that is reason to rejoice!

Be my strength. Be my portion. Be my life. Be my joy. Be my all in all. In Jesus' name, Amen.

Day 36—Zephaniah

God Rejoices Over You

The Lord your God in your midst,
The Mighty One, will save;
He will rejoice over you with gladness,
He will quiet you with His love,
He will rejoice over you with singing.
(Zeph. 3:17, NKJV)

Prayer

Lord, You are the God who sees me, knows me, loves me, and dwells with me.

You drew us to Yourself through the sacrifice of Your Son, Jesus Christ. You provide. You save. You rejoice over us with gladness, for we are Your very own people bought with the blood of Christ.

When we are afraid, You quiet us with Your love. With You in our midst, there is nothing to fear. We hear Your attentive Father's voice singing over us, and we are brought to tears.

It amazes us to think that One so great, so holy, and so good would set His affections on mortal ones such as us—so small, so frail, so needy.

We are overwhelmed at Your love, pouring down like a waterfall, drenching our souls with life-giving, heavenly love. May Your love song echo in our hearts and minds. No matter what happens, we are loved by the Creator of the universe. We are loved! In Jesus' name, Amen.

Day 37—Haggai

God Is Worthy of an Acceptable Offering

> Then the word of the Lord came by the hand of Haggai the prophet, "Is it a time for you yourselves to dwell in your paneled houses, while this house lies in ruins? Now, therefore, thus says the Lord of hosts: Consider your ways. You have sown much, and harvested little. You eat, but you never have enough; you drink, but you never have your fill. You clothe yourselves, but no one is warm. And he who earns wages does so to put them into a bag with holes.
>
> "Thus says the Lord of hosts: Consider your ways. Go up to the hills and bring wood and build the house, that I may take pleasure in it and that I may be glorified, says the Lord. You looked for much, and behold, it came to little. And when you brought it home, I blew it away. Why? declares the Lord of hosts. Because of my house that lies in ruins, while each of you busies himself with his own house." (Hag. 1:3–9, ESV)

Prayer

Lord God, You are robed in majesty and armed with strength. Your throne was established from before time. You are from all eternity. How glorious the splendor of Your beauty and grace. We see Your magnificence in the sparkling blue skies, the glowing white moon, the patterns on the wings of the butterfly, and the joy in every smiling face. The beauty of Your artistry outweighs a million shining gems. You deserve our adoration and praise!

May we not neglect the care of Your earthly work, for through it we accomplish Your spiritual work. Help us to not neglect Your church while we care for our homes. Give us generous hearts to bring You an offering worthy of Your great name. You invite us to help bear the glory of Your kingdom. Let us know the depths of this sacred privilege.

We thank You, Lord Almighty, for Your Spirit is among us, and Your glory is in our midst. May Your beauty emanate from Your people. May we glow with the light of Christ. May we stop at nothing to bring forth Your kingdom plans in us and through us. For Your glory, for Your kingdom, for the excellence of Your name! In Jesus' name, Amen.

ঔ

Day 38—Zechariah

God Moves Mountains by His Spirit

> Then he said to me, "This is the word of the Lord to Zerubbabel: Not by might, nor by power, but by my Spirit, says the Lord of hosts. Who are you, O great mountain? Before Zerubbabel you shall become a plain. And he shall bring forward the top stone amid shouts of 'Grace, grace to it!'" (Zech. 4:6–7, ESV)

Prayer

Lord of hosts, how great You are. The weight of mountains is nothing to You. The ocean depths are but a drop to You. You are Lord of all. You are God, and You are Spirit.

As we carry out Your mighty kingdom work, help us remember that we accomplish nothing in our own strength. Your work is completed not by might, nor by power, but by Your Spirit alone. You have the capacity to create and re-create every atom and molecule of Your vast creation.

Whatever mountains stand before us, we call on the grace of Christ. His grace is greater than all our sins, than all our failures, than all our weaknesses.

Spirit of the Living God, fall afresh on us. Move any mountains that hold us back from loving You. We give full access to Your Spirit to bring forth every gift You placed within us. Let our lives be an offering to You and a blessing to Your world. In Jesus' name, Amen.

ᔓ

Day 39—Malachi

God Remembers Those Who Revere Him

> For I the Lord do not change; therefore you, O children of Jacob, are not consumed. From the days of your fathers you have turned aside from my statutes and have not kept them. Return to me, and I will return to you, says the Lord of hosts. (Mal. 3:6–7, ESV)
>
> Then those who feared the Lord spoke with one another. The Lord paid attention and heard them, and a book of remembrance was written before him of those who feared the Lord and esteemed his name. "They shall be mine, says the Lord of hosts, in the day when I make up my treasured possession, and I will spare them as a man spares his son who serves him. Then once more you shall see the distinction between the righteous and the wicked, between one who serves God and one who does not serve him. (3:16–18, ESV)

Prayer

Eternal God, You are the LORD who does not change. From everlasting to everlasting, You are God. Your statutes stand firm. Holiness adorns Your house forever. Every Word You have spoken will come to pass. Every mercy in Christ and every judgment against sin will stand.

Your integrity and purity are absolute. You are endowed with incomparable might. You are God and is there is no other. Give us a revelation of Your glory, Your greatness, and Your flawless perfection, so we gain a proper fear and rightful reverence of You.

May we be found in Your book of remembrance. May we turn to Christ and be saved, all the ends of the earth. For without You, we are nothing.

Have mercy on us, Lord. We are sinners in need of a Savior.

Through Christ's grace, we know our names are recorded in Your book of remembrance. Remember us, Your sons and daughters in Christ. Remember us in Your mercy and grace. Remember us, as You remembered the thief on the cross near You. When we take our last breath, may we hear the words, "Well done, My good and faithful servant. Enter into your rest." In Jesus' name, Amen.

ഗ

New Testament Scriptures and Prayers

Day 40—Matthew

Jesus Christ Is Savior and Lord

Now the birth of Jesus Christ took place in this way. When his mother Mary had been betrothed to Joseph, before they came together she was found to be with child from the Holy Spirit. (Matt. 1:18, ESV)

From that time Jesus began to preach, saying, "Repent, for the kingdom of heaven is at hand." (4:17, ESV)

Jesus went throughout Galilee, teaching in their synagogues, proclaiming the good news of the kingdom, and healing every disease and sickness among the people. (4:23, NIV)

And the high priest said to him, "I adjure you by the living God, tell us if you are the Christ, the Son of God." Jesus said to him, "You have said so. But I tell you, from now on you will see the Son of Man seated at the right hand of Power and coming on the clouds of heaven." Then the high priest tore his robes and said, "He has uttered blasphemy. What further witnesses do we need? You have now heard his blasphemy. What is your judgment?" They answered, "He deserves death." (26:63–66, ESV)

Then the soldiers of the governor took Jesus into the governor's headquarters, and they gathered the whole battalion before him. And they stripped him and put a scarlet robe on him, and twisting together a crown of thorns, they put it on his head and put a reed in his right hand. And kneeling before him, they mocked him, saying, "Hail, King of the Jews!" And they spit on him and took the reed and struck him on the head. And when they had mocked him, they stripped him of the robe and put his own clothes on him and led him away to crucify him. (Matt. 27:27–31, ESV)

Now after the Sabbath, toward the dawn of the first day of the week, Mary Magdalene and the other Mary went to see the tomb. And behold, there was a great earthquake, for an angel of the Lord descended from heaven and came and rolled back the stone and sat on it. His appearance was like lightning, and his clothing white as snow. And for fear of him the guards trembled and became like dead men. But the angel said to the women, "Do not be afraid, for I know that you seek Jesus who was crucified. He is not here, for he has risen, as he said. Come, see the place where he lay. Then go quickly and tell his disciples that he has risen from the dead, and behold, he is going before you to Galilee; there you will see him. (28:1–7, ESV)

And Jesus came and said to them, "All authority in heaven and on earth has been given to me. Go therefore and make disciples of all nations, baptizing them in the name of the Father and of the Son and of the Holy Spirit, teaching them to observe all that I have commanded you. And behold, I am with you always, to the end of the age." (28:18–20, ESV)

Prayer

Jesus Christ, Savior of the world, You are Lord! Thank You for coming down from heaven, fully God and fully man. You walked among us and took our sins on Your shoulders. You paid the penalty for our sins and rose again in all power and authority.

Then You ascended into heaven,
sent Your Holy Spirit to indwell the hearts of all who believe,
and You intercede for us from Your heavenly throne,
until that day when You come again

to judge the living and the dead,
and rule and reign forever.

You are above all and beyond all. We worship at Your feet. You rescued us from hell, You cleansed us of all sin, and You won us for heaven. Oh, what a Savior!

The One who made the Garden laid down His life to restore us, so we could join Him in the heavenly garden. We yearn to see You by the river and tree in the new heavens and the new earth. From creation to re-creation, You are the Master Healer.

For all eternity, we will sing Your praises as we gaze upon the glory of God in the face of Christ! Help us this day to live a life that is worthy of Your precious name! In Jesus' name, Amen.

Day 41—Mark

Jesus Christ Is the Son of God

> That day when evening came, he [Jesus] said to his disciples, "Let us go over to the other side." Leaving the crowd behind, they took him along, just as he was, in the boat. There were also other boats with him. A furious squall came up, and the waves broke over the boat, so that it was nearly swamped. Jesus was in the stern, sleeping on a cushion. The disciples woke him and said to him, "Teacher, don't you care if we drown?"
>
> He got up, rebuked the wind and said to the waves, "Quiet! Be still!" Then the wind died down and it was completely calm.
>
> He said to his disciples, "Why are you so afraid? Do you still have no faith?"
>
> They were terrified and asked each other, "Who is this? Even the wind and the waves obey him!" (Mark 4:35–41, NIV)

> Again the high priest asked him, "Are you the Messiah, the Son of the Blessed One?"
>
> "I am," said Jesus. "And you will see the Son of Man sitting at the right hand of the Mighty One and coming on the clouds of heaven."
>
> The high priest tore his clothes. "Why do we need any more witnesses?" he asked. "You have heard the blasphemy. What do you think?"
>
> They all condemned him as worthy of death. Then some began to spit at him; they blindfolded him, struck him with their fists, and said, "Prophesy!" And the guards took him and beat him. (Mark 14:61–65, NIV)

Prayer

Jesus Christ, You are God from the beginning. The wind and the waves already know Your voice and obey Your every command. You, who walked on the water, will walk one day on the clouds of heaven when You usher in the new heaven and earth.

As we face the storms of life that swirl and rock our boats, help us sense the indwelling Spirit of God, the One who spoke all things into existence, the One who lives inside our hearts.

Through the tears, sweat, and blood that streamed down Your body on the cross, You saw us. We were Your joy. Help us to see past the darkness of this world that threatens to grip our hearts and see You up ahead, waiting for us in the heavenly realms to welcome us home. Help us to remember that You are our joy.

Son of God and Son of man, Savior of the world, Savior of my soul—oh, how I love You! In Your name, Amen.

ᔕ

Day 42—Luke

Jesus Christ Forgives Sins

And there were shepherds living out in the fields nearby, keeping watch over their flocks at night. An angel of the Lord appeared to them, and the glory of the Lord shone around them, and they were terrified. But the angel said to them, "Do not be afraid. I bring you good news that will cause great joy for all the people. Today in the town of David a Savior has been born to you; he is the Messiah, the Lord. This will be a sign to you: You will find a baby wrapped in cloths and lying in a manger."

Suddenly a great company of the heavenly host appeared with the angel, praising God and saying,

"Glory to God in the highest heaven,
and on earth peace to those on whom his favor rests."

When the angels had left them and gone into heaven, the shepherds said to one another, "Let's go to Bethlehem and see this thing that has happened, which the Lord has told us about."

So they hurried off and found Mary and Joseph, and the baby, who was lying in the manger. When they had seen him, they spread the word concerning what had been told them about this child, and all who heard it were amazed at what the shepherds said to them. (Luke 2:8–18, NIV)

When one of the Pharisees invited Jesus to have dinner with him, he went to the Pharisee's house and reclined at the table. A woman in that town who lived a sinful life learned that Jesus was eating at the Pharisee's house, so she came there with an alabaster jar of perfume. As she stood behind him at his feet weeping, she began to wet his feet with her tears. Then she wiped them with her hair, kissed them and poured perfume on them.

When the Pharisee who had invited him saw this, he said to himself, "If this man were a prophet, he would know who is touching him and what kind of woman she is—that she is a sinner."

Jesus answered him, "Simon, I have something to tell you."

"Tell me, teacher," he said.

"Two people owed money to a certain moneylender. One owed him five hundred denarii, and the other fifty. Neither of them had the money to pay him back, so he forgave the debts of both. Now which of them will love him more?"

Simon replied, "I suppose the one who had the bigger debt forgiven."

"You have judged correctly," Jesus said.

Then he turned toward the woman and said to Simon, "Do you see this woman? I came into your house. You did not give me any water for my feet, but she wet my feet with her tears and wiped them with her hair. You did not give me a kiss, but this woman, from the time I entered, has not stopped kissing my feet. You did not put oil on my head, but she has poured perfume on my feet. Therefore, I tell you, her many sins have been forgiven—as her great love has shown. But whoever has been forgiven little loves little."

Then Jesus said to her, "Your sins are forgiven."

The other guests began to say among themselves, "Who is this who even forgives sins?"

Jesus said to the woman, "Your faith has saved you; go in peace." (Luke 7:36–50, NIV)

Two other men, both criminals, were also led out with him to be executed. When they came to the place called the Skull, they crucified him there, along with the criminals—one on his right, the other on his left. Jesus said, "Father, forgive them, for they do not know what they are doing." (23:32–34, NIV)

Prayer

Lord Jesus, all glory to Your great name! Glory to God in the highest! King of the world, You were sent to save us from the beginning.

You left the heavenly realms where all the angels sing Your praises. You humbled Yourself, taking the form of a child, wrapping Yourself in a cloak of humanity, so we could not see Your deity. You walked among us, You taught us your truth and exposed our self-exalting ways.

God of heaven, You bore the sins of the people You made. What amazing grace! What amazing mercy! What amazing love!

Not because we are so good, or so faithful, or so worthy, but because You are so good, so faithful, and so worthy!

May we bow low, washing Your nail-scarred feet with our tears, drying Your feet with our hair. Lamb of God, slain for the sins of the world.

God of creation, You redeemed the world with Your own blood.

King of heaven, You absorbed the penalty for the rebellion of humanity.

Jesus Christ is the One who pays for my sins, the One who forgives my sins.

Glory to God in the highest!

Peace on earth to those on whom His favor rests!

Peace with God, for my sins no longer separate me from my Creator.

Peace with God. Peace now and forever. In Jesus' name, Amen.

Day 43—John

Jesus Christ Is the Way, the Truth, and the Life

> In the beginning was the Word, and the Word was with God, and the Word was God. He was in the beginning with God. All things were made through Him, and without Him nothing was made that was made. (John 1:1–3, NKJV)
>
> For God so loved the world that He gave His only begotten Son, that whoever believes in Him should not perish but have everlasting life. For God did not send His Son into the world to condemn the world, but that the world through Him might be saved.
>
> He who believes in Him is not condemned; but he who does not believe is condemned already, because he has not believed in the name of the only begotten Son of God. (3:16–18, NKJV)
>
> It was just before the Passover Festival. Jesus knew that the hour had come for him to leave this world and go to the Father. Having loved his own who were in the world, he loved them to the end. (13:1, NIV)
>
> Jesus said to him, "I am the way, the truth, and the life. No one comes to the Father except through Me." (14:6, NKJV)

Prayer

Jesus Christ, You are The Word. The Creator. God from the beginning. You are part of the triune Godhead, the Trinity:

> *God the Father,*
> *God the Son,*
> *God the Spirit.*

Jesus Christ, You are God's Word, God's communication, God's message, God's living truth.

Jesus Christ, You came to save—to be God's in-person communication.

Jesus Christ, You came to love and to die, to seek and save the lost.

A sacrifice of immeasurable value was required to atone for sins against an immeasurable God. So Jesus Christ, God in flesh, willingly absorbed the just penalty for our sins.

There is no other way. There is no other truth. There is no other life without Jesus Christ.

Jesus, forever, we praise Your glorious name! In Your name, Amen.

Day 44—Acts

The Holy Spirit Indwells Believers

> And while staying with them he [Jesus] ordered them [the disciples] not to depart from Jerusalem, but to wait for the promise of the Father, which, he said, "you heard from me; for John baptized with water, but you will be baptized with the Holy Spirit not many days from now."
>
> So when they had come together, they asked him, "Lord, will you at this time restore the kingdom to Israel?" He said to them, "It is not for you to know times or seasons that the Father has fixed by his own authority. But you will receive power when the Holy Spirit has come upon you, and you will be my witnesses in Jerusalem and in all Judea and Samaria, and to the end of the earth." And when he had said these things, as they were looking on, he was lifted up, and a cloud took him out of their sight. And while they were gazing into heaven as he went, behold, two men stood by them in white robes, and said, "Men of Galilee, why do you stand looking into heaven? This Jesus, who was taken up from you into heaven, will come in the same way as you saw him go into heaven." (Acts 1:4–11, ESV)

> And Peter said to them, "Repent and be baptized every one of you in the name of Jesus Christ for the forgiveness of your sins, and you will receive the gift of the Holy Spirit. (Acts 2:38, ESV)
>
> And they [Paul and Silas] said, "Believe in the Lord Jesus, and you will be saved, you and your household." (16:31, ESV)

Prayer

Holy Spirit, thank You for the favor of Your comforting, strengthening presence within. You are the Breath of God and Spirit of our resurrected Savior. Without your indwelling power, we could not live fully for Christ.

Holy Spirit, You are our Teacher, our Guide, our Counselor, the One who corrects and disciplines us, our Purifier, our Sanctifier, our Healer. You are the strength of Almighty God within our very frame.

Oh, what a wonder, that in these cracked earthen vessels, we carry the treasure of heaven! Thank You for this astounding privilege, Jesus.

We invite You, Holy Spirit, to do your heavenly work in our innermost being. Prune the sins that hold us back from Christ. Nourish us with the living water of Christ and the daily bread of Your Word. Illuminate Your Word as we read. Teach us the ways we should go.

May we grow in the fruit of the Spirit: love, joy, peace, patience, kindness, goodness, faithfulness, gentleness, and self-control. Remind us that we cannot merely drum up these qualities ourselves. These godly traits are grown as we abide in the True Vine, Jesus Christ.

Reignite our hunger to read the Bible. Renew our spirits as we praise You in song. Revitalize and refresh us as we spend time in prayer, communing with our Heavenly Father and our Lord Jesus, through the power of the Holy Spirit within.

May we be found worthy of Your great name! Do a mighty, miraculous work in our hearts, minds, and lives. We love You, Jesus, and we want to live in a way that shows that we do! In Your name, Amen.

Day 45—Romans

Jesus Christ Saves Sinners

For all have sinned and fall short of the glory of God. (Rom. 3:23, ESV)

But God demonstrates his own love for us in this: While we were still sinners, Christ died for us. (5:8, NIV)

For the wages of sin is death, but the free gift of God is eternal life in Christ Jesus our Lord. (6:23, ESV)

If you confess with your mouth that Jesus is Lord and believe in your heart that God raised him from the dead, you will be saved. (10:9, ESV)

For "everyone who calls on the name of the Lord will be saved." (10:13, ESV)

Prayer

Heavenly Father, we sing praises to Your name! Your glory, Your holiness, Your purity, and Your truth shine into the darkness of our sinful, selfish hearts with a piercing and penetrating light. We acknowledge that we are sinners desperately in need of a Savior.

Thank You, precious Jesus, for while our backs were turned to You, You were pouring out Your blood on the cross for us.

To cover us with your mercy and grace.
To wrap us in Your robe of righteousness.

Now our sins are canceled forever by Your sacrificial blood.

Taking our place.
Taking our penalty.
Exchanging it all for your holiness and grace.

Thank You for this incredible gift. We confess that Jesus is Lord and believe in our hearts that God raised Him from the dead. By faith in Your finished work on the cross we are saved.

We cannot earn it. We do not deserve it. There is nothing we can do to repay You. It is the grace and mercy of heaven, pouring down like a river upon us.

There is only one condition: All we must do is confess and believe. We are saved by grace through faith.

As our hearts overflow with gratitude, we pray to live a life worthy of Your name. Holy Spirit, empower us to follow Christ and His Word.

May our hearts burst with joy, for we are saved! We are free! We are made new in Christ forever! In Jesus' name, Amen.

ꟹ

Day 46—First Corinthians

God Is Love

> If I speak in the tongues of men and of angels, but have not love, I am a noisy gong or a clanging cymbal. And if I have prophetic powers, and understand all mysteries and all knowledge, and if I have all faith, so as to remove mountains, but have not love, I am nothing. If I give away all I have, and if I deliver up my body to be burned, but have not love, I gain nothing.
>
> Love is patient and kind; love does not envy or boast; it is not arrogant or rude. It does not insist on its own way; it is not irritable or resentful; it does not rejoice at wrongdoing, but rejoices with the truth. Love bears all things, believes all things, hopes all things, endures all things.
>
> Love never ends. As for prophecies, they will pass away; as for tongues, they will cease; as for knowledge, it will pass away. For we know in part and we prophesy in part, but when the perfect comes, the partial will pass away. When I was a child, I spoke like a child, I thought like a child, I reasoned like a child.

When I became a man, I gave up childish ways. For now we see in a mirror dimly, but then face to face. Now I know in part; then I shall know fully, even as I have been fully known.

So now faith, hope, and love abide, these three; but the greatest of these is love. (1 Cor. 13:1–13, NIV)

Now, brothers and sisters, I want to remind you of the gospel I preached to you, which you received and on which you have taken your stand. By this gospel you are saved, if you hold firmly to the word I preached to you. Otherwise, you have believed in vain.

For what I received I passed on to you as of first importance: that Christ died for our sins according to the Scriptures, that he was buried, that he was raised on the third day according to the Scriptures, and that he appeared to Cephas [Peter], and then to the Twelve. After that, he appeared to more than five hundred of the brothers and sisters at the same time, most of whom are still living, though some have fallen asleep. (15:3–6, NIV)

Prayer

Heavenly Father, You are love. Without You, we would not know what love is. Through the gift of Your Son, Jesus Christ, we see what real love looks like. This is not the world's definition of love, which is lustful and self-oriented.

Your love is sacrificial. Your love is based on purity, truth, and righteousness.

Your love looks like a King of heaven, walking on the earth He made, dying for the people He created, so we could be part of Your kingdom family. That is love.

Your love is not selfish. Your love is not prideful or arrogant. Your love is truthful and merciful. Your love endures.

Holy Spirit, fill us with the love of Jesus, a divine love that is beyond us. When we think of love, give us a vision of Jesus on the cross.

Remind us of His love, drenching us with blood-red truth, justice, and mercy.

Give us a heart like Jesus' heart. Help us to exude His love. Let them know we are Christians by our love. In Jesus' name, Amen.

ഗ

Day 47—Second Corinthians

Power Belongs to God

> For God, who said, "Let light shine out of darkness," has shone in our hearts to give the light of the knowledge of the glory of God in the face of Jesus Christ.
>
> But we have this treasure in jars of clay, to show that the surpassing power belongs to God and not to us. We are afflicted in every way, but not crushed; perplexed, but not driven to despair; persecuted, but not forsaken; struck down, but not destroyed; always carrying in the body the death of Jesus, so that the life of Jesus may also be manifested in our bodies. (2 Cor. 4:6–10, ESV)
>
> So we do not lose heart. Though our outer self is wasting away, our inner self is being renewed day by day. For this light momentary affliction is preparing for us an eternal weight of glory beyond all comparison, as we look not to the things that are seen but to the things that are unseen. For the things that are seen are transient, but the things that are unseen are eternal. (4:16–18, ESV)

Prayer

Wonderful God, Your light shines into our hearts, enabling us to see Your glory in the face of Christ! We are now flooded with His light, beaming out through all our cracks. As the world beholds Your radiance glowing through our flaws and frailties, may they recognize You as the source.

Let our faith remain steadfast, despite hardships, sorrows, difficulties, and persecution. Our faith in the Risen Lord is not crushed, no matter what befalls us in this world. For we remember this world is not our home.

Reshape us through every teardrop that falls. As we release each burden to You, we are being matured, letting go of this life, and clinging tighter to Christ. Give us spiritual vision to perceive every element of this world as fading before our very eyes, while the light of eternity blazes more brightly with each passing day. Anchor our very beings in the truth that what is unseen is actually eternal. In Jesus' name, Amen.

Day 48—Galatians

Walk by the Spirit

> But I say, walk by the Spirit, and you will not gratify the desires of the flesh. For the desires of the flesh are against the Spirit, and the desires of the Spirit are against the flesh, for these are opposed to each other, to keep you from doing the things you want to do. But if you are led by the Spirit, you are not under the law. Now the works of the flesh are evident: sexual immorality, impurity, sensuality, idolatry, sorcery, enmity, strife, jealousy, fits of anger, rivalries, dissensions, divisions, envy, drunkenness,

orgies, and things like these. I warn you, as I warned you before, that those who do such things will not inherit the kingdom of God. But the fruit of the Spirit is love, joy, peace, patience, kindness, goodness, faithfulness, gentleness, self-control; against such things there is no law. And those who belong to Christ Jesus have crucified the flesh with its passions and desires.

If we live by the Spirit, let us also keep in step with the Spirit. (Gal. 5:16–25, ESV)

Prayer

Father God, fill us afresh with Your Holy Spirit. Help us to live in ways that honor You. We see how much our fleshly bodies desire things of this world. Daily we battle against our selfish desires. Greed, envy, impure thoughts, sensual or sexual desires that are not aligned with Your Word, anger, drunkenness, pride, making idols of money, jobs, status or relationships, and all manner of things that go against Your Word. How easy it is to slip back into these sinful habits and ways of thinking.

Help us, Holy Spirit, to walk in new ways—ways that look and sound like Jesus, who was perfectly holy and perfectly loving. Dig up the soil of our hearts, pulling out roots of sin.

Plant the seeds of Your Word deep within. Add the Son-light of Christ, the refreshment of Your Spirit and the dew of God's heavenly love. Cause us to grow in the fruit of the Spirit. May we produce a great harvest of righteousness as a blessing to You and to the world. Cultivate in us Your love, joy, peace, patience, kindness, goodness, faithfulness, gentleness, and self-control. Help us exude Christ's beauty in this sin-burdened world. In Jesus' name, Amen.

ꕥ

Day 49—Ephesians

Put On the Armor of God

But God, being rich in mercy, because of the great love with which he loved us, even when we were dead in our trespasses, made us alive together with Christ—by grace you have been saved— and raised us up with him and seated us with him in the heavenly places in Christ Jesus, so that in the coming ages he might show the immeasurable riches of his grace in kindness toward us in Christ Jesus. For by grace you have been saved through faith. And this is not your own doing; it is the gift of God, not a result of works, so that no one may boast. For we are his workmanship, created in Christ Jesus for good works, which God prepared beforehand, that we should walk in them. (Eph. 2:4–10, ESV)

Finally, be strong in the Lord and in the strength of his might. Put on the whole armor of God, that you may be able to stand against the schemes of the devil. For we do not wrestle against flesh and blood, but against the rulers, against the authorities, against the cosmic powers over this present darkness, against the spiritual forces of evil in the heavenly places. Therefore take up the whole armor of God, that you may be able to withstand in the evil day, and having done all, to stand firm. Stand therefore, having fastened on the belt of truth, and having put on the breastplate of righteousness, and, as shoes for your feet, having put on the readiness given by the gospel of peace. In all circumstances take up the shield of faith, with which you can extinguish all the flaming darts of the evil one; and take the helmet of salvation, and the sword of the Spirit, which is the word of God, praying at all times in the Spirit, with all prayer and supplication. (6:10–18, ESV)

Prayer

Almighty God, thank You for the mercy and love You extend to us through Jesus Christ. We are alive in Christ through Your grace. Call forth every gift You have placed in us, to use for Your glory and to uplift Your people. May we complete the good works You planned for us. May we display Your divine craftsmanship.

Strengthen us, Holy Spirit. Empower and embolden us with the breath of Almighty God. Stir our minds and prick our hearts to put on the armor of God, much like we put on our clothes to prepare for the day ahead.

Place in the forefront of our minds that our true enemy is Satan and his demonic forces. Help us to recall with sober mind that Satan is real, and is powerful—but that no one is more powerful than YOU.

Help us, with serious minds, to buckle ourselves with Your truth, and wrap ourselves in the righteousness Christ won for us. Help us step into the shoes that proclaim His gospel of good news. Wherever we walk, help us appeal to people with the message that Jesus saves.

As we secure our shield of faith, bring remembrances of Your sovereign power. We arm ourselves with Christ's victory and authority, knowing our salvation in Him is firm and unshakable. Our salvation is not our making, but Yours.

Help us carry within us and before us the Word of God. Empower us to speak Your truth over every lie of the enemy. Give us prayerful hearts, led by the Holy Spirit. Lift our heads, for we walk not in our own strength, but in the strength of Yahweh, the great I AM—today and always. In Jesus' name, Amen.

ຯ

Day 50—Philippians

Jesus Christ, Name Above All Names

> Have this mind among yourselves, which is yours in Christ Jesus, who, though he was in the form of God, did not count equality with God a thing to be grasped, but emptied himself, by taking the form of a servant, being born in the likeness of men. And being found in human form, he humbled himself by becoming obedient to the point of death, even death on a cross. Therefore God has highly exalted him and bestowed on him the name that is above every name, so that at the name of Jesus every knee should bow, in heaven and on earth and under the earth, and every tongue confess that Jesus Christ is Lord, to the glory of God the Father. (Phil. 2:5–11, ESV)
>
> Rejoice in the Lord always; again I will say, rejoice. Let your reasonableness be known to everyone. The Lord is at hand; do not be anxious about anything, but in everything by prayer and supplication with thanksgiving let your requests be made known to God. And the peace of God, which surpasses all understanding, will guard your hearts and your minds in Christ Jesus.
>
> Finally, brothers, whatever is true, whatever is honorable, whatever is just, whatever is pure, whatever is lovely, whatever is commendable, if there is any excellence, if there is anything worthy of praise, think about these things. What you have learned and received and heard and seen in me—practice these things, and the God of peace will be with you. (4:4–9, ESV)

Prayer

Jesus Christ, we exalt You! Lamb of God, we exalt You! Savior of the world, we exalt You! King of Kings and Lord of Lords, we exalt You! There is power in the name of Jesus! You have defeated Satan, sin, hell, and death forever! Blessed be Your glorious name!

Lord Jesus, we are thrilled to be in Your family. You displayed obedience to the Father on the cross. You embodied humility, justice, and mercy. We are overwhelmed by Your love and grace!

Whether we are on the mountaintop or in the valley, let our hearts rejoice, for we are found in Christ! Whether we have much or we have little, help us to rest in the peace You gained for us on the cross. Our hearts are made right before God, and we have peace with God forever. That is reason to rejoice, no matter how dark the clouds overhead.

May we run to You with our prayers and leave them at the foot of the cross, remembering that You have already defeated the greatest evil there ever was or ever will be. Help us to release our burdens into Your gentle and strong hands. Cover us in Your peace, which passes all understanding. Guard our hearts and minds in Christ Jesus.

Let our thoughts return to You again and again, remembering all that You are—goodness, purity, truth, justice, righteousness, love, excellence, honor. Let our hearts and minds swirl around the beauty of Your character and gaze upon the lovely facets of Your nature that sparkle like diamonds glittering in the light of day.

When our thoughts drift to evil or sadness or distractions—or ourselves—shake us and reset our minds on Christ. Let the wonder of heaven envelop us and hold our hearts close to You, for you are good. You are awesome; You are worthy of our utmost worship. In Your name, Amen.

Day 51—Colossians

Jesus Christ Is Preeminent, God the Son

And so, from the day we heard, we have not ceased to pray for you, asking that you may be filled with the knowledge of his will in all spiritual wisdom and understanding, so as to walk in a manner worthy of the Lord, fully pleasing to him: bearing fruit in every good work and increasing in the knowledge of God; being strengthened with all power, according to his glorious might, for all endurance and patience with joy; giving thanks to the Father, who has qualified you to share in the inheritance of the saints in light. He has delivered us from the domain of darkness and transferred us to the kingdom of his beloved Son, in whom we have redemption, the forgiveness of sins.

He [Jesus Christ] is the image of the invisible God, the firstborn of all creation. For by him all things were created, in heaven and on earth, visible and invisible, whether thrones or dominions or rulers or authorities—all things were created through him and for him. And he is before all things, and in him all things hold together. And he is the head of the body, the church. He is the beginning, the firstborn from the dead, that in everything he might be preeminent. For in him all the fullness of God was pleased to dwell, and through him to reconcile to himself all things, whether on earth or in heaven, making peace by the blood of his cross. (Col. 1:9–20, ESV)

Prayer

Jesus Christ, how we praise You! You brought us out of darkness into Your marvelous light. What a gift! A blessing like no other. You have redeemed us and transformed us through the forgiveness of sins. Because of You, Jesus, and Your ultimate sacrifice, now we share in the inheritance of heaven.

Your amazing love is magnified even more, as we remember that You are God, the triune Godhead: God the Father, God the Son, God the Spirit. You are the image of the invisible God. All things were made through You and for You. You are before all, beyond all, above all, and You hold all things together. You created all life, died for our sins, then rose up again, demonstrating Your power over death. You are Preeminent over all!

Creator God, You absorbed into Yourself the penalty for our sins, reconciling us back to Yourself. You made us in love; You died for us in love; You brought us back to Yourself in love. Enlarge our hearts to love like You, our Savior, our God, and our King. In Your name, Amen.

Day 52—First Thessalonians

God Sanctifies Us

> For the Lord himself will descend from heaven with a cry of command, with the voice of an archangel, and with the sound of the trumpet of God. And the dead in Christ will rise first. Then we who are alive, who are left, will be caught up together with them in the clouds to meet the Lord in the air, and so we will always be with the Lord. Therefore encourage one another with these words. (1 Thess. 4:16–18, ESV)

> Rejoice always, pray without ceasing, give thanks in all circumstances; for this is the will of God in Christ Jesus for you. Do not quench the Spirit. Do not despise prophecies, but test everything; hold fast what is good. Abstain from every form of evil.

> Now may the God of peace himself sanctify you completely, and may your whole spirit and soul and body be kept blameless at the coming of our Lord Jesus Christ. He who calls you is faithful; he will surely do it. (5:16–24, ESV)

Prayer

Lord Jesus, help us remember, no matter the darkness that surrounds us, You are coming again! All who have faith in You will be caught up together with You forever. May we eagerly look forward to that day and say to each other, "Jesus is coming back for us! Maybe it is today!" Help us to encourage our hearts in You.

Holy Spirit, teach us Your ways. Infuse us with Your Word. Engulf our hearts with love for our Savior. Revive us again this day. Give us wisdom and discernment to warn those who are off track, to encourage those who are downtrodden, and to help those who are hurting. Help us show patience to everyone we may meet. Help us to remember that each person is fighting a battle we do not know.

Let the joy of our salvation bubble over and cascade into the world. Prompt our minds to return to prayer again and again. Give us hearts of thanksgiving for the rich blessings from our Father. If we are awake and breathing, this is God's first miracle of today, for we cannot cause our heart to beat even one more time. Moment by moment, help us to remember Your great faithfulness.

Purify us, sanctify us, cleanse us. Carve us into the image of Christ, bit by bit and day by day. Protect our hearts and minds. Keep up blameless before the coming of our Lord Jesus Christ. Not by our efforts, but as we lean into You. We can count on You. You are powerful. You are able, Mighty God. You are the One who called us into Your kingdom family. You are the One who will keep us on the narrow path. In Jesus' name, Amen.

Day 53—Second Thessalonians

Jesus Christ Will Return as Judge

This is evidence of the righteous judgment of God, that you may be considered worthy of the kingdom of God, for which you are also suffering—since indeed God considers it just to repay with affliction those who afflict you, and to grant relief to you who are afflicted as well as to us, when the Lord Jesus is revealed from heaven with his mighty angels in flaming fire, inflicting vengeance on those who do not know God and on those who do not obey the gospel of our Lord Jesus. They will suffer the punishment of eternal destruction, away from the presence of the Lord and from the glory of his might, when he comes on that day to be glorified in his saints, and to be marveled at among all who have believed, because our testimony to you was believed. To this end we always pray for you, that our God may make you worthy of his calling and may fulfill every resolve for good and every work of faith by his power, so that the name of our Lord Jesus may be glorified in you, and you in him, according to the grace of our God and the Lord Jesus Christ. (2 Thess. 1:5–12, ESV)

Now concerning the coming of our Lord Jesus Christ and our being gathered together to him, we ask you, brothers, not to be quickly shaken in mind or alarmed, either by a spirit or a spoken word, or a letter seeming to be from us, to the effect that the day of the Lord has come. Let no one deceive you in any way. For that day will not come, unless the rebellion comes first, and the man of lawlessness is revealed, the son of destruction, who opposes and exalts himself against every so-called god or object of worship, so that he takes his seat in the temple of God, proclaiming himself to be God. Do you not remember that when I was still with you I told you these things? And you know what is restraining him now so that he may be revealed in his time. For the mystery of lawlessness is already at work. Only he who now restrains it will do so until he is out of the way. And then the lawless one will be revealed, whom the Lord Jesus will kill with the breath of his mouth and bring to nothing by the appearance of his coming. The coming of the lawless one is by the activity of Satan with all power and false signs and wonders, and with all wicked deception for those who are perishing, because they refused to love the truth and so be saved. Therefore God sends them a strong delusion, so that they may believe what is false, in order that all may be condemned who did not believe the truth but had pleasure in unrighteousness. (2 Thess. 2:1–10, ESV)

Prayer

Lord Jesus, we exalt Your great name! You are Savior, King, and Judge. Just as every prophecy of Your first coming was fulfilled, so will every prophecy of Your second coming be fulfilled. For You spoke and it came to be. Your Word is final.

Heavenly Father, keep us abiding in You and marveling at Your righteousness and mercy. Let the name of Jesus Christ be glorified and magnified through our lives. Purify us by the power of Your indwelling Holy Spirit, that we may be found worthy of our King when He returns to judge the living and the dead.

Holy Spirit, give us discernment in these evil and dark times. Help us to not be deceived by any false teacher or anyone who exalts their word over Your Word, the Bible.

Set divine appointments for us to tell others about the gospel of Jesus Christ, for the hour is late. He can save to the uttermost.

May we rest in the truth of Your Word and the power of Your name, Jesus Christ. You provided us with these end times prophecies, so we would be prepared, not scared. We are sheltered under the saving power of Jesus Christ. We are cleansed by His blood and held in His faithful hands—now and forever. In Jesus' name, Amen.

Day 54—First Timothy

Christ Is the Mediator Between God and Mankind

> First of all, then, I urge that supplications, prayers, intercessions, and thanksgivings be made for all people, for kings and all who are in high positions, that we may lead a peaceful and quiet life, godly and dignified in every way. This is good, and it is pleasing in the sight of God our Savior, who desires all people to be saved and to come to the knowledge of the truth. For there is one God, and there is one mediator between God and men, the man Christ Jesus, who gave himself as a ransom for all, which is the testimony given at the proper time. (1 Tim. 2:1–6, ESV)

Prayer

Heavenly Father, Your leadership in our lives is a blessing. We are also grateful for the earthly leaders You provide for us. Anoint them to lead with wisdom, truth, and grace.

You desire all people to be saved and come to a knowledge of the truth. May Your Word and Your Spirit go forth in power this day, opening blind eyes and unstopping deaf ears, that more people would believe in Jesus as Savior and Lord.

Jesus, how we thank You for all You have done. You are fully God and fully man. You know what it is like to be tempted. Yet You were without sin. You left the glory of heaven in order to walk among us in the flesh. You walked with us in dirt, dust, blood, sweat, and tears. You know our sorrows and have experienced our earthly pain.

Jesus, You did not stand back. You entered into our suffering. You are the suffering Savior.

Only you are fit to mediate between a holy God and a sinful people.

As our Mediator, our Advocate, our Counselor, You paid our ransom. You are like a lawyer in the courtroom who stepped forward and paid the penalty for the guilty one charged with a death sentence. You accepted the just judgment against us so we could go free. Every debt was paid in full with Your precious blood. God's justice was upheld, and then You poured mercy from the floodgates of heaven upon us—upon any who will believe and call You Lord.

Our Mediator became our Savior and then rose again as KING and Judge. We are in awe of Your great love and mercy toward us. There is none like You! In Your name, Amen.

Day 55—Second Timothy

All Scripture Is From God

All Scripture is God-breathed and is useful for teaching, rebuking, correcting and training in righteousness, so that the servant of God may be thoroughly equipped for every good work. (2 Tim. 3:16, NIV)

I charge you in the presence of God and of Christ Jesus, who is to judge the living and the dead, and by his appearing and his kingdom: preach the word; be ready in season and out of season; reprove, rebuke, and exhort, with complete patience and teaching. For the time is coming when people will not endure sound teaching, but having itching ears they will accumulate for themselves teachers to suit their own passions, and will turn away from listening to the truth and wander off into myths. As for you, always be sober-minded, endure suffering, do the work of an evangelist, fulfill your ministry. (4:1–5, ESV)

Christ Awards a Crown of Righteousness

I have fought the good fight, I have finished the race, I have kept the faith. Henceforth there is laid up for me the crown of righteousness, which the Lord, the righteous judge, will award to me on that day, and not only to me but also to all who have loved his appearing. (2 Tim. 4:7–8, ESV)

Prayer

Almighty God, You spoke, and the universe took its shape. You commanded, and it stood firm. Your Word is life. Your Word is truth. Your Word stands forever. Heaven and earth will pass away, but your Word will never pass away.

Ignite in us deep desire to read Your Word. To ponder, understand, know, and memorize Your Word. Holy Spirit, teach us the deep meaning. Clarify parts that are difficult to comprehend. Help us to consume and absorb Your Word into every fiber of our being. Change us as we read and listen. Help us desire the things You desire, think Your thoughts, walk in Your ways, and pray the prayers of Your heart. Let Your Word take us over, Holy Spirit.

Thank You, Lord Jesus, You have purchased for us the crown of righteousness. We are made right with God by Your blood. May our love for You expand as we await Your return. May we be found faithful until that day when You take us home. The crowns You won for us, we will present back to You, and lay at Your feet. Worthy is the Lamb slain for the sins of the world! Holy, Holy, Holy are You! In Your name, Amen.

Day 56—Titus

We Are a People for God's Own Possession

> For the grace of God has appeared, bringing salvation for all people, training us to renounce ungodliness and worldly passions, and to live self-controlled, upright, and godly lives in the present age, waiting for our blessed hope, the appearing of the glory of our great God and Savior Jesus Christ, who gave himself for us to redeem us from all lawlessness and to purify

for himself a people for his own possession who are zealous for good works. (Titus 2:11–14, ESV)

For we ourselves were once foolish, disobedient, led astray, slaves to various passions and pleasures, passing our days in malice and envy, hated by others and hating one another. But when the goodness and loving kindness of God our Savior appeared, he saved us, not because of works done by us in righteousness, but according to his own mercy, by the washing of regeneration and renewal of the Holy Spirit, whom he poured out on us richly through Jesus Christ our Savior, so that being justified by his grace we might become heirs according to the hope of eternal life. (Titus 3:3–7, ESV)

Prayer

Father God, as we await our blessed hope, the return of Jesus Christ our Lord, may we live in a way that exudes the fragrance of heaven, that demonstrates for a watching world what it means to be a member of God's family.

What a precious gift to be God's possession! We are loved by God in Jesus Christ, and so we love You in return. Help us to live like we love YOU!

Give us grace toward others as we remember we were once lost, disobedient, and rebellious toward You. By your grace, O Lord, our Savior came. Not because we are so good, but because You are so good. Thank You, Holy Spirit, for washing us, regenerating us, remaking us into the image of Christ. We are heirs of His kingdom, heaven-bound heirs, joyfully treasuring each day with the hope of life everlasting in Christ. May our hope and joy spring eternal! In Jesus' name, Amen.

ꙮ

Day 57—Philemon

We Are Brothers and Sisters in Christ

> Accordingly, though I am bold enough in Christ to command you to do what is required, yet for love's sake I prefer to appeal to you—I, Paul, an old man and now a prisoner also for Christ Jesus— I appeal to you for my child, Onesimus, whose father I became in my imprisonment. (Formerly he was useless to you, but now he is indeed useful to you and to me.) I am sending him back to you, sending my very heart. I would have been glad to keep him with me, in order that he might serve me on your behalf during my imprisonment for the gospel, but I preferred to do nothing without your consent in order that your goodness might not be by compulsion but of your own accord. For this perhaps is why he was parted from you for a while, that you might have him back forever, no longer as a bondservant but more than a bondservant, as a beloved brother—especially to me, but how much more to you, both in the flesh and in the Lord.
>
> So if you consider me your partner, receive him as you would receive me. (Philem. 1:8–17, ESV)

Prayer

Heavenly Father, give us Your vision to see other believers as brothers and sisters in Christ. Grant us eyes like Paul to look upon other believers as family. For this earthly structure is passing away and one day soon we will all gather, bowing low at the feet of Christ our Savior. Help us to link arms now, one in the Spirit, one in the Lord, as one family of faith.

Whether we were given high status and responsibilities in this life or lowly, humble positions, may we see one another as made in the image of God, precious in the sight of God, blood-bought brothers and sisters in the kingdom of God. May this world have no hold on our love or respect for one another.

May Your divine love connect us heart to heart and hand to hand until that day when we are gathered together before Your throne. Help us to consider ourselves privileged to be servants of the Most High God. In Jesus' name, Amen.

Day 58—Hebrews

Jesus Christ Upholds the Universe

Long ago, at many times and in many ways, God spoke to our fathers by the prophets, but in these last days he has spoken to us by his Son, whom he appointed the heir of all things, through whom also he created the world. He is the radiance of the glory of God and the exact imprint of his nature, and he upholds the universe by the word of his power. After making purification for sins, he sat down at the right hand of the Majesty on high, having become as much superior to angels as the name he has inherited is more excellent than theirs. (Heb. 1:1–4, ESV)

Jesus Christ Is Our High Priest

For the word of God is living and active, sharper than any two-edged sword, piercing to the division of soul and of spirit, of joints and of marrow, and discerning the thoughts and intentions of the heart. And no creature is hidden from his sight, but all are naked and exposed to the eyes of him to whom we must give account.

Since then we have a great high priest who has passed through the heavens, Jesus, the Son of God, let us hold fast our confession. For we do not have a high priest who is unable to sympathize with our weaknesses, but one who in every respect has been tempted as we are, yet without sin. Let us then with confidence draw near to the throne of grace, that we may receive mercy and find grace to help in time of need. (Heb. 4:12–16, ESV)

Prayer

Christ Jesus, we exalt You! You embody the brilliance of God's glory. You uphold the universe by Your eternal Word. You are majestic, glorious, high and lifted up!

Your Word is powerful. Your Word is living. As we read the Bible, by the power of Your Holy Spirit, it reads us. You pierce through every nuance of self-deception, self-righteousness, self-aggrandizement. Nothing is hidden from Your blazing light of truth. All are laid bare before You, the One to whom we must give an account.

Thank You, Jesus, Son of God, for You are also the High Priest. You go before our Holy God to present a worthy sacrifice for our sins, the sacrifice of Your own Holy blood.

You are a High Priest who knows what it is like to be tempted by sin, and yet You knew no sin. Because You know us, and You paid for our sin-darkened hearts with Your pure heart, we can draw near without fear. We are sanctified by Your blood, which speaks a better word over our lives. That word is mercy.

Because of You, Jesus, our Sacrificial Lamb and High Priest, we can enter into the Holy of Holies. We advance into unhindered closeness with our Creator God and Abba Father. Because of You, we are made perfect and spotless.

We enter with confidence in You, Jesus. And in You, we find mercy, grace, and help in our time of need. You are always there. In Your name, Amen.

Day 59—James

Faith Is Evidenced in Good Works

> What good is it, my brothers, if someone says he has faith but does not have works? Can that faith save him? If a brother or sister is poorly clothed and lacking in daily food, and one of you says to them, "Go in peace, be warmed and filled," without giving them the things needed for the body, what good is that? So also faith by itself, if it does not have works, is dead. (James 2:14–17, ESV)
>
> Therefore confess your sins to each other and pray for each other so that you may be healed. The prayer of a righteous person is powerful and effective. (5:16, NIV)

Prayer

Holy Spirit, stir up within us a true and living faith in Jesus Christ. We cannot earn our way to heaven. Rather, we are saved by grace through faith in Jesus Christ.

We acknowledge that true faith includes a changed heart and a changed mind. This results in a changed life. A life that reflects the goodness, purity, and love of our Savior.

Help us live out our faith in real time so others may see our good works and glorify our Father in heaven. May we be the hands and feet of Jesus to the people around us. Help us to give evidence of our faith by walking the walk, not just talking the talk. Let our faith result in visible, Christlike words and actions. Let Jesus be glorified and lived out through us!

As part of our transformed lives, help us to be honest about our sin struggles. Help us confess our shortcomings and wrong choices and ask others to pray for us. The prayers of those made righteous in Christ are powerful and can move mountains, just as Jesus said! Help us to humble ourselves before God and one another and PRAY! For you are faithful and just to forgive us our sins and cleanse us of all unrighteousness. Thank you, Lord, for fresh, daily cleansing. In Jesus' name, Amen.

Day 60—First Peter

We Are God's Special People

> But you are a chosen generation, a royal priesthood, a holy nation, His own special people, that you may proclaim the praises of Him who called you out of darkness into His marvelous light; who once were not a people but are now the people of God, who had not obtained mercy but now have obtained mercy. (1 Pet. 2:9–10, NKJV)
>
> He himself bore our sins in his body on the tree, that we might die to sin and live to righteousness. By his wounds you have been healed. (2:24, ESV)
>
> Clothe yourselves, all of you, with humility toward one another, for "God opposes the proud but gives grace to the humble."
>
> Humble yourselves, therefore, under the mighty hand of God so that at the proper time he may exalt you, casting all your anxieties on him, because he cares for you. Be sober-minded; be watchful. Your adversary the devil prowls around like a roaring lion, seeking someone to devour. Resist him, firm in your faith, knowing that the same kinds of suffering are being experienced by your brotherhood throughout the world. And after you have suffered a little while, the God of all grace, who has called you to his eternal glory in Christ, will himself restore, confirm, strengthen, and establish you. To him be the dominion forever and ever, Amen. (5:5–11, ESV)

Prayer

Heavenly Father, our hearts erupt with gratitude. You have chosen us to be Your own special people. By grace we are saved and made new in Christ Jesus. We are born again, brought into Your marvelous light through the mercy of Christ's sacrifice on the cross.

Thank You, Lord Jesus. You carried our sins, and they were nailed to the cross. By Your wounds our sin-sick souls are healed.

May we now live our lives as sons and daughters of the Most High God, worthy of this high calling. For we are a royal priesthood, a holy nation, set apart to glorify and worship You. May we look to the cross and remember the mercy shed for us. Keep us humble before You.

Help us to be watchful, knowing that Satan, the enemy of our souls, is after every follower of Jesus to turn them away. We pray against the devil and cancel all his wicked schemes. Lord, we rebuke Satan. We declare that Jesus Christ is LORD! Holy Spirit, strengthen us to resist the devil and run to Jesus. Be our sword and shield. May we walk in righteousness, for Your name's sake. May Your truth ever light our way. In Jesus' name, Amen.

❧

Day 61—Second Peter

God Is Patient

> But do not overlook this one fact, beloved, that with the Lord one day is as a thousand years, and a thousand years as one day. The Lord is not slow to fulfill his promise as some count slowness, but is patient toward you, not wishing that any should perish, but that all should reach repentance. But the day of the Lord will come like a thief, and then the heavens will pass away with a roar, and the heavenly bodies will be burned up and dissolved, and the earth and the works that are done on it will be exposed.
>
> Since all these things are thus to be dissolved, what sort of people ought you to be in lives of holiness and godliness, waiting for and hastening the coming of the day of God, because of which the heavens will be set on fire and dissolved, and the heavenly bodies will melt as they burn! But according to his promise we are waiting for new heavens and a new earth in which righteousness dwells. (2 Pet. 3:8–13, ESV)

Prayer

Heavenly Father, You have patiently drawn us to Yourself, softening our stony hearts to accept the gift of salvation in Christ. Give us patience as You work in the lives of others. You are gentle and speak in that still small voice. You call each one by name, asking them to repent from sin and turn to Christ.

Day by day, You whisper through the song of the birds in the morning and the twinkle of stars at night. In a million ways, big and small, You display Your glory. You remind us there is something more. You call us to know our Creator and Savior.

O Lord, our hearts ache along with Yours at those who refuse to come to You. We stand in the gap today for those who are lost from Your fold. May their hearts yield to You this day. Let them run to the Great Shepherd's arms, safe from evil, both within and without.

Holy Spirit, help us take seriously our own salvation. Inflame our hearts anew. Help us to earnestly endeavor to live in holiness and godliness, for we do not know when the day of the LORD will occur. Reinvigorate us with joy. Reignite our fervency to pray for others. Each day is one day closer to the new heavens and earth where only righteousness will dwell. We long for that day, Lord! Keep us strong in Christ. In His name, Amen.

Day 62—First John

God Forgives

If we confess our sins, he is faithful and just to forgive us our sins and to cleanse us from all unrighteousness. (1 John 1:9, ESV)

God Loves

We love Him because He first loved us. (4:19, NKJV)

God Helps Us Obey and Overcome

Everyone who believes that Jesus is the Christ has been born of God, and everyone who loves the Father loves whoever has been born of him. By this we know that we love the children of God, when we love God and obey his commandments. For this is the love of God, that we keep his commandments. And his commandments are not burdensome. For everyone who has been born of God overcomes the world. And this is the victory that has overcome the world—our faith. Who is it that overcomes the world except the one who believes that Jesus is the Son of God? (5:1–5, ESV)

Prayer

Gracious God, thank You. You forgave and cleansed us at salvation and we are cleansed each day, as we confess our sins and turn to You in honesty and humility. Thank You for loving us. As Your love rushes in, we are saturated and well up with holy love for You and for others. Thank You for this blessing of divine, unending, unconditional love.

You demonstrated Your love for us, not by feelings, but through Christ's actions on the cross. Help us demonstrate our love for You by obeying Your Word. Your commands are not a burden, but come from Your heart of goodness, justice, holiness, righteousness, and purity.

Help us overcome this world by our faith. Not by our might, not by our power, but by Your Spirit which indwells us. Let our faith be strengthened as we read your Word, connect with You in prayer, and sing praises to You from the heart. We are overcomers, because we have faith in Jesus who overcame it all! Thank You, Jesus! In Your name, Amen.

ග

Day 63—Second John

Abide in God's Word for a Full Reward

> For many deceivers have gone out into the world, those who do not confess the coming of Jesus Christ in the flesh. Such a one is the deceiver and the antichrist. Watch yourselves, so that you may not lose what we have worked for, but may win a full reward. Everyone who goes on ahead and does not abide in the teaching of Christ, does not have God. Whoever abides in the teaching has both the Father and the Son. (2 John 1:7–9, ESV)

Prayer

Holy Spirit, tether our hearts and minds to the truth of Your Word. May we not be led astray by the voice of a stranger or deceiver. Plant Your Word so deep in our hearts that the roots cannot be shaken by this world or anyone in it.

Help us abide in the teaching of Christ, our True Vine. Without the truth of Your Word, we do not have God. As we believe and follow Your Word, which stands forever, we have the blessing of God.

We desire to honor the God who spoke us into existence,

the God who provided His written Word,

the God who spoke "It is finished" on the cross,

the God who waits up ahead in heaven,

ready to reward all who believe in Jesus Christ,

who died for our sins and rose again in all power, authority and dominion,

and now is seated at the right hand of the throne of God in heaven.

Father, Son, and Spirit.

Let nothing move our hearts and minds from the truth of Your Word, for we are like the flowers that fade in the autumn winds—but your Word stands forever. Help us stand with You. In Jesus' name, Amen.

ఆ

Day 64—Third John

Walk in the Truth

> Beloved, I pray that you may prosper in all things and be in health, just as your soul prospers. For I rejoiced greatly when brethren came and testified of the truth that is in you, just as you walk in the truth. I have no greater joy than to hear that my children walk in truth. (3 John 1:2–4, NKJV)

Prayer

Holy Spirit, help us walk in the truth. Not the opinions of our neighbors, family, friends, or culture. Not the ebb and flow of our feelings and circumstances, but Your eternal truth—God's Word.

May Your truth be written on the pages of our hearts. May Your truth soak into every fiber of our beings. May Your truth point us to the narrow road that leads to Christ. May Your truth set us free from all sin and self-deception. May we bring joy to You, heavenly Father, as we walk in the truth and help others join us.

Stir up in us a desire for absolute truth. If we seek absolute truth, we will find Jesus. Jesus is the way, the truth, and the life. No one comes to the Father but by Him. Jesus, thank You for teaching us the truth of Your Word and embodying truth in Your very being. In Your name, Amen.

Day 65—Jude

Keep Yourself in the Love of God

> But you must remember, beloved, the predictions of the apostles of our Lord Jesus Christ. They said to you, "In the last time there will be scoffers, following their own ungodly passions." It is these who cause divisions, worldly people, devoid of the Spirit. But you, beloved, building yourselves up in your most holy faith and praying in the Holy Spirit, keep yourselves in the love of God, waiting for the mercy of our Lord Jesus Christ that leads to eternal life. And have mercy on those who doubt; save others by snatching them out of the fire; to others show mercy with fear, hating even the garment stained by the flesh.
>
> Now to him who is able to keep you from stumbling and to present you blameless before the presence of his glory with great joy, to the only God, our Savior, through Jesus Christ our Lord, be glory, majesty, dominion, and authority, before all time and now and forever. Amen. (Jude 1:17–24, ESV)

Prayer

Holy Spirit, build up our most holy faith as we read and listen to Your Word. Faith comes by hearing and hearing by the Word of God. Strengthen us in our innermost beings, Almighty God. Anchor our hearts and minds in Your truth. Jesus is the way, the truth, and the life.

As we remember Jesus, we remember Your great love and mercy raining down upon us at the cross. We wait with assurance for our glorious eternal life in Christ.

Give us tender, compassionate hearts toward those who doubt You, Lord. Help us to lead them away from fiery, hell-bound choices in direct opposition to You. May we lead with truth, mercy, love, reverential fear, and awe.

Fear of the Lord is the beginning of wisdom, and we do not wish to be swept up into the sinful choices of others. As we reach a helping hand to those caught in sin, may we not be pulled into sin ourselves. Help us remain strong in Christ, with our feet planted on the Rock of ages.

You alone, Lord Jesus, are able to keep us from stumbling, to keep us blameless and in right standing before our Holy God. You alone, Christ Jesus, hold the glory, majesty, power, and authority from all eternity. Hallelujah, we are safe in Your hands! In Your name, Amen.

Day 66—Revelation

He Will Reign Forever and Ever

> After this I looked, and behold, a great multitude that no one could number, from every nation, from all tribes and peoples and languages, standing before the throne and before the Lamb, clothed in white robes, with palm branches in their hands, and crying out with a loud voice, "Salvation belongs to our God who sits on the throne, and to the Lamb!" And all the angels were standing around the throne and around the elders and the four living creatures, and they fell on their faces before the throne and worshiped God, saying, "Amen! Blessing and glory and wisdom and thanksgiving and honor and power and might be to our God forever and ever! Amen." (Rev. 7:9–12, ESV)
>
> Now I saw heaven opened, and behold, a white horse. And He who sat on him was called Faithful and True, and in righteousness He judges and makes war. His eyes were like a flame of fire, and on His head were many crowns. He had a name written that no one knew except Himself. He was clothed with a robe dipped in blood, and His name is called The Word of God. And the armies in heaven, clothed in fine linen, white and clean, followed Him on white horses. Now out of His mouth goes a sharp sword, that with it He should strike the nations. And He Himself will rule them with a rod of iron. He Himself treads the winepress of the fierceness and wrath of Almighty God. And He has on His robe and on His thigh a name written:
>
> KING OF KINGS AND
> LORD OF LORDS.
>
> (19:11–16, NKJV)

Then I saw a new heaven and a new earth, for the first heaven and the first earth had passed away, and the sea was no more. And I saw the holy city, new Jerusalem, coming down out of heaven from God, prepared as a bride adorned for her husband. And I heard a loud voice from the throne saying, "Behold, the dwelling place of God is with man. He will dwell with them, and they will be his people, and God himself will be with them as their God. He will wipe away every tear from their eyes, and death shall be no more, neither shall there be mourning, nor crying, nor pain anymore, for the former things have passed away."

And he who was seated on the throne said, "Behold, I am making all things new." Also he said, "Write this down, for these words are trustworthy and true." And he said to me, "It is done! I am the Alpha and the Omega, the beginning and the end. To the thirsty I will give from the spring of the water of life without payment. The one who conquers will have this heritage, and I will be his God and he will be my son. But as for the cowardly, the faithless, the detestable, as for murderers, the sexually immoral, sorcerers, idolaters, and all liars, their portion will be in the lake that burns with fire and sulfur, which is the second death."(Rev. 21:1–8, ESV)

And he showed me a pure river of water of life, clear as crystal, proceeding from the throne of God and of the Lamb. In the middle of its street, and on either side of the river, was the tree of life, which bore twelve fruits, each tree yielding its fruit every month. The leaves of the tree were for the healing of the nations. And there shall be no more curse, but the throne of God and of the Lamb shall be in it, and His servants shall serve Him. They shall see His face, and His name shall be on their foreheads. There shall be no night there: They need no lamp nor light of the sun, for the Lord God gives them light. And they shall reign forever and ever. (22:1–5, NKJV)

He who testifies to these things says, "Surely I am coming quickly."

Amen. Even so, come, Lord Jesus! (22:20, NKJV)

Prayer

Hallelujah to the KING OF KINGS! Hallelujah to the LORD OF LORDS! Hallelujah to the Most High God, who rules and reigns! He is seated forever on His throne of righteousness and justice!

Holy, holy, holy are You, Lord God Almighty!

You are the Alpha and the Omega, the First and the Last, the Beginning and the End. Jesus Christ, You are the Author and Finisher of our faith.

At Your first coming, You were the sacrificial Lamb of God, slain for the sins of the world. But You will return as the Lion of the Tribe of Judah, making war and defeating all who oppose You. Satan and all evil will be stamped out forever. No more sin. No more sorrow. No more suffering.

As declared from the beginning, when Adam and Eve were cast out of the Garden of Eden, an offspring of the woman would crush the head of the serpent. Now we know the Savior's name is Jesus.

As foretold from the beginning, in the book of Genesis, people from every nation, tribe, and language will be part of Your kingdom family. From Abraham, all nations of the world are blessed!

As promised in Your Word, all who repent and believe Jesus is Lord will be rescued from hell, cleansed of all sin, and invited into the heavenly family of God. The One who gave us life laid down His life that we could have eternal life in His presence.

Let praises erupt from our souls! Jesus Christ has won! Jesus Christ is victorious! Jesus Christ is LORD!

Come, Lord Jesus!

We say, yes! Amen!

ɞ

Appendix A

A One-Year Bible Reading Plan

DESPITE MY unsuccessful attempt to read through the Bible with my kids (as I described in Chapter 1), I still believe in reading the whole Bible—and doing it in one year is a reasonable goal. All that is needed is a simple, flexible plan.

The plan on the next four pages is nothing more than a check-off chart with every chapter of the Bible. If you read three to four chapters a day (three on weekdays and four on Saturday and Sunday, for instance), you will complete the entire Bible in a single year. Feel free to photocopy these pages on the front and back of a single sheet of paper, and use it for a bookmark.

The beauty of this plan is that it is so flexible—you don't need to start at Genesis and finish with Revelation; you can move around. Although I enjoy reading straight through the Bible, I also read sometimes in the Old Testament, sometimes in the New Testament; I mix my reading of historical books like First and Second Kings with poetical books like Psalms and Proverbs, and pastoral instruction, such as Paul's letters to the Corinthians, Ephesians, and Colossians.

Because an *average* of three to four chapters is my daily goal, I can feel free to limit my reading one day to two long chapters (such as in Genesis or Exodus), while another day I might read an entire book of five shorter chapters (such as James or First Peter). Think of this as an adventure, not a legalism—if you miss a day, you can simply pick up where you left off, and not worry about having to "catch up" to a structured schedule.

I invite you to take on this challenge—you'll never regret it!

Genesis

1 2 3 4 5 6 7 8 9 10 11 12 13
14 15 16 17 18 19 20 21 22 23
24 25 26 27 28 29 30 31 32 33
34 35 36 37 38 39 40 41 42 43
44 45 46 47 48 49 50

Exodus

1 2 3 4 5 6 7 8 9 10 11 12 13
14 15 16 17 18 19 20 21 22 23
24 25 26 27 28 29 30 31 32 33
34 35 36 37 38 39 40

Leviticus

1 2 3 4 5 6 7 8 9 10 11 12 13
14 15 16 17 18 19 20 21 22 23
24 25 26 27

Numbers

1 2 3 4 5 6 7 8 9 10 11 12 13
14 15 16 17 18 19 20 21 22 23
24 25 26 27 28 29 30 31 32 33
34 35 36

Deuteronomy

1 2 3 4 5 6 7 8 9 10 11 12
13 14 15 16 17 18 19 20 21
22 23 24 25 26 27 28 29 30
31 32 33 34

Joshua

1 2 3 4 5 6 7 8 9 10 11 12
13 14 15 16 17 18 19 20 21
22 23 24

Judges

1 2 3 4 5 6 7 8 9 10 11 12
13 14 15 16 17 18 19 20 21

Ruth

1 2 3 4

1st Samuel

1 2 3 4 5 6 7 8 9 10 11 12 13
14 15 16 17 18 19 20 21 22 23
24 25 26 27 28 29 30 31

2nd Samuel

1 2 3 4 5 6 7 8 9 10 11 12
13 14 15 16 17 18 19 20 21
22 23 24

1st Kings

1 2 3 4 5 6 7 8 9 10 11 12 13
14 15 16 17 18 19 20 21 22

2nd Kings

1 2 3 4 5 6 7 8 9 10 11 12
13 14 15 16 17 18 19 20 21
22 23 24 25

1st Chronicles

1 2 3 4 5 6 7 8 9 10 11 12 13
14 15 16 17 18 19 20 21 22 23
24 25 26 27 28 29

2nd Chronicles

1 2 3 4 5 6 7 8 9 10 11 12 13
14 15 16 17 18 19 20 21 22 23
24 25 26 27 28 29 30 31 32 33
34 35 36

Ezra
1 2 3 4 5 6 7 8 9 10

Nehemiah
1 2 3 4 5 6 7 8 9 10 11 12 13

Esther
1 2 3 4 5 6 7 8 9 10

Job
1 2 3 4 5 6 7 8 9 10 11 12 13
14 15 16 17 18 19 20 21 22 23
24 25 26 27 28 29 30 31 32 33
34 35 36 37 38 39 40 41 42

Psalms
1 2 3 4 5 6 7 8 9 10 11 12 13
14 15 16 17 18 19 20 21 22 23
24 25 26 27 28 29 30 31 32 33
34 35 36 37 38 39 40 41 42 43
44 45 46 47 48 49 50 51 52 53
54 55 56 57 58 59 60 61 62 63
64 65 66 67 68 69 70 71 72 73
74 75 76 77 78 79 80 81 82 83
84 85 86 87 88 89 90 91 92 93
94 95 96 97 98 99 100 101 102
103 104 105 106 107 108 109
110 111 112 113 114 115 116
117 118 119 120 121 122 123
124 125 126 127 128 129 130
131 132 133 134 135 136 137
138 139 140 141 142 143 144
145 146 147 148 149 150

Proverbs
1 2 3 4 5 6 7 8 9 10 11 12 13
14 15 16 17 18 19 20 21 22 23
24 25 26 27 28 29 30 31

Ecclesiastes
1 2 3 4 5 6 7 8 9 10 11 12

Song of Solomon
1 2 3 4 5 6 7 8

Isaiah
1 2 3 4 5 6 7 8 9 10 11 12 13
14 15 16 17 18 19 20 21 22 23
24 25 26 27 28 29 30 31 32 33
34 35 36 37 38 39 40 41 42 43
44 45 46 47 48 49 50 51 52 53
54 55 56 57 58 59 60 61 62 63
64 65 66

Jeremiah
1 2 3 4 5 6 7 8 9 10 11 12 13
14 15 16 17 18 19 20 21 22 23
24 25 26 27 28 29 30 31 32 33
34 35 36 37 38 39 40 41 42 43
44 45 46 47 48 49 50 51 52

Lamentations
1 2 3 4 5

Ezekiel
1 2 3 4 5 6 7 8 9 10 11 12 13
14 15 16 17 18 19 20 21 22 23
24 25 26 27 28 29 30 31 32 33
34 35 36 37 38 39 40 41 42 43
44 45 46 47 48

Daniel

1 2 3 4 5 6 7 8 9 10 11 12

Hosea

1 2 3 4 5 6 7 8 9
10 11 12 13 14

Joel

1 2 3

Amos

1 2 3 4 5 6 7 8 9

Obadiah

1

Jonah

1 2 3 4

Micah

1 2 3 4 5 6 7

Nahum

1 2 3

Habakkuk

1 2 3

Zephaniah

1 2 3

Haggai

1 2

Zechariah

1 2 3 4 5 6 7 8 9
10 11 12 13 14

Malachi

1 2 3 4

Matthew

1 2 3 4 5 6 7 8 9 10 11 12
13 14 15 16 17 18 19 20 21
22 23 24 25 26 27 28

Mark

1 2 3 4 5 6 7 8 9 10
11 12 13 14 15 16

Luke

1 2 3 4 5 6 7 8 9 10 11 12
13 14 15 16 17 18 19 20 21
22 23 24

John

1 2 3 4 5 6 7 8 9 10 11 12
13 14 15 16 17 18 19 20 21

Acts

1 2 3 4 5 6 7 8 9 10 11 12
13 14 15 16 17 18 19 20 21
22 23 24 25 26 27 28

Romans

1 2 3 4 5 6 7 8 9 10
11 12 13 14 15 16

1st Corinthians

1 2 3 4 5 6 7 8 9 10
11 12 13 14 15 16

2nd Corinthians

1 2 3 4 5 6 7 8
9 10 11 12 13

Galatians

1 2 3 4 5 6

Ephesians

1 2 3 4 5 6

Philippians

1 2 3 4

Colossians

1 2 3 4

1st Thessalonians

1 2 3 4 5

2nd Thessalonians

1 2 3

1st Timothy

1 2 3 4 5 6

2nd Timothy

1 2 3 4

Titus

1 2 3

Philemon

1

Hebrews

1 2 3 4 5 6 7 8
9 10 11 12 13

James

1 2 3 4 5

1st Peter

1 2 3 4 5

2nd Peter

1 2 3

1st John

1 2 3 4 5

2nd John

1

3rd John

1

Jude

1

Revelation

1 2 3 4 5 6 7 8 9 10
11 12 13 14 15 16 17
18 19 20 21 22

Appendix B

Bible Reading Guidelines

WHEN READING the Bible, keep in mind the following six guidelines to enhance your understanding.

1. Remember the Goal

The goal of reading the Bible is to know God and His love for us and to love Him in response. Our relationship with God is strengthened through reading and studying His Word.

God has revealed Himself to us through creation, through the Bible, through His Son, and through His Spirit. God has spoken to us specifically and intentionally through His Word, the Bible. What a privilege to hear from the God of the universe! Therefore, the Bible is worthy of our study and contemplation.

Knowing God means knowing His Word.

We can't have a relationship with anyone unless we spend time together and communicate with each other. As we pray, we are talking to God. As we read the Bible, God is speaking to us. Unless we read His Word and understand the depths of His love through Christ, we are missing out on the greatest love we will ever know.

2. Have a Humble Heart

Approach Bible reading with a humble heart and a teachable spirit. We must remember that the God of all creation has spoken. The Bible contains His Word. Our goal is to know Him—to know His will and His way, and not to misuse His Word to support our desires. God loves us with a purifying love. If we come to Him with a softened and surrendered heart, the door of our soul is opened for God to express His truth, love, and grace in ways that transform us into the image of Christ.

3. Get Help from the Best Teacher

Pray and ask the Holy Spirit to teach you and make the Bible come alive as you read. We all benefit from inviting the Holy Spirit to illuminate the Scriptures as we read.

The Bible is God's written Word. Jesus is God's Living Word. The indwelling Holy Spirit is the presence of God alive in the hearts of believers. The Spirit of God is within us! When we request the Spirit to move and work in us, He exposes deep parts of our souls and reveals things we cannot perceive for ourselves.

The Holy Spirit knows the mind of God and can teach us unfathomable divine truth from His Word. The Holy Spirit can highlight verses that speak uniquely to our present situations, bringing healing, strength, hope, peace, conviction, and wisdom to our lives. Let's pause, pray, and ask the Holy Spirit to teach us and bring the Bible to life as we read.

4. Keep in Mind the Big Picture

Stand back and view the Bible as a whole. Although the Bible includes 66 books, it contains one unifying theme. After reading *The Whole Bible Devotional*, you know the theme of the Bible is Jesus. From Genesis to Revelation, the Bible reveals God's amazing plan to redeem His people through Jesus' sacrifice on the cross and resurrection from the grave.

Though we may focus on a particular book, chapter, or verse when reading, we must also keep Jesus at the forefront as the ultimate main message. This helps to anchor every other part.

5. Take a Closer Look

Read in context. When you read a passage or verse, be sure to view that section in context. Some Bibles offer a brief overview at the beginning of each book. Understanding the background and setting of a book lays a solid foundation when seeking the accurate meaning of a given verse. In addition, read the verses and paragraphs before and after each section, so phrases or sentences are not taken out of context.

The point of reading the Bible is to know God. The intent is not to add our thoughts and commentaries to God's truth but to allow His truth to inform and transform us. Reading in context is key to comprehending and understanding God's life-changing message.

6. Think Deeply

Consider the biblical principle from the passage. Though some sections of Scripture are written for certain people at a certain point in time, there are general principles that can be applied to any person at any time. This requires deeper thinking.

For example, though Job's story of suffering was from a far different era, a period when most people survived on personal livestock and crops, we certainly can still appreciate the agony of losing one's livelihood and wondering where the next meal is coming from. Learning to trust God, even when we can't understand our circumstances, is a timeless lesson from the story of Job.

Godly wisdom can be learned from every book of the Bible if we pause, pray, and ponder.

Here are some questions to ask as you read:

1. What does this passage reveal about God's nature and character?
2. What does this passage convey about the Savior?
3. What does this passage teach about my need for a Savior and my identity in Christ?
4. Does this passage spotlight any changes needed in my life to become more like Jesus?

As you read and endeavor to understand the Bible, may these six guidelines deepen your engagement with God and His Word.

1. Keep in mind the goal of Bible reading: to know God and His love, and to love Him in return.
2. Approach the Bible with a humble heart.
3. Pray before you begin, asking the Holy Spirit to make God's Word come alive.
4. Remember the main message of the Bible is Jesus. God redeems His fallen people through Christ. God loves you! Consider how shorter passages fit into this overall theme.
5. Read passages of the Bible in context.
6. Think deeply about biblical principles that apply to your life today.

By reading the Bible in this way, you can:

- Get to know the heart and will of the Father.
- Get to know the love of the Savior who leads with nail-scarred hands.
- Get to know the voice of the Spirit—that still, small voice within who calls to us day after day.

A Bible Reading Prayer

Speak, O God, through your Word and your Spirit.

Speak, O God, and reveal your Son, our Savior.

Speak, O God, into our hearts with your truth, grace, and love.

Speak, O God, for your servants are listening.

Speak, O God, for your Word is life.

Specific Bible Reading Tips

Below are several tips for reading the Bible. I hope you find these strategies helpful as you deepen your faith in Christ by reading His Word.

On a Personal Note

My husband and I enjoy reading the Bible in a year and do so frequently. As mentioned in the Bible Reading Plan, by reading three or four chapters per day, you can read the whole Bible in a year. This kind of large sweep reading enables you to track the flow of the biblical narrative and find connecting points. If you have never read the Bible in a year, I encourage you to try. You'll be glad you did!

However, there is also merit to reading slowly, taking notes, meditating on the Scriptures, and doing a deeper study of a particular book of the Bible. This in-depth method of Bible reading unfolds layers of beauty as you absorb the Scriptures thoroughly. Sometimes I take a break from reading the Bible in a year and focus on a particular book study.

Both types of Bible reading are important. Reading the entire Bible paints a complete picture of God's grace in Christ. Alternatively, gazing intently at one book of the Bible spotlights the astounding details in Scripture. As you continue your Bible reading journey, I pray you avail yourself of all the treasures found there.

Rule of Thumb When Reading the Bible in a Year

Reading about three chapters a day is a good general rule if you want to get through the whole Bible in a year. However, you might want to consider the number of verses in a chapter if you want to avoid feeling overwhelmed by excessively long chapters.

For those who love numbers, you need to read about 85 verses a day to get through the Bible in a year. To clarify this point, if you read the first three chapters of Luke, you'll read 170 verses—twice as many verses as the daily average. On the other hand, if you read Psalms 1, 2, and 3, you've read three "chapters," but only 26 verses.

Therefore, you may choose to pace yourself by the number of verses read rather than the number of chapters. Either way, it's helpful to keep in mind that one chapter of the Bible may be significantly shorter or longer than another, which will affect the amount of time needed to read this portion. Give yourself grace if more time is needed or if you need to pick up another day to finish reading.

Tackling Difficult Parts of Scripture

As you read the Bible, it is important to note that some parts of Scripture are harder to read than others. However, that depends on the person. Some people find historical books like First and Second Kings hard to follow, while others get bogged down by the Psalms, because poetic language is just not their "thing." The prophets are difficult reading for some people, because it's not always easy to understand the specific situation the prophet is addressing.

A little historical and cultural research helps a lot in these cases. For these difficult chapters, I read the notes in my study Bible, check out Bible commentaries, or search for other trusted biblical sources to provide the background I need.

Pausing to gain some historical and cultural context enriches your reading, especially with the challenging sections.

Encountering Difficult Names

Names of people and places in the Bible are sometimes troublesome to pronounce. These names originate from a different language and century. Therefore, some of these names are seldom heard apart from the Bible.

If you encounter a name that begins with the letter "A" followed by ten or twelve letters you cannot pronounce, I recommend simply replacing that name (in your head) with "Person A."

While reading, it might sound like this in your mind: "Person A and Person R went to City H."

There is no need to let complex biblical names hinder your reading or intimidate you from continuing.

Bible Translations

The goal of reading anything is to comprehend what the author is communicating. The goal of reading the Bible is to grasp the meaning of God's Word. Be sure to choose a Bible translation you can understand. Many people love the older Bible translations and that is fine. However, if you cannot make sense of the text, you are defeating the purpose. Select a Bible translation that is clear and understandable to you.

Is This Your First Time Reading the Bible?

If you are reading the Bible for the very first time, I recommend beginning in the New Testament with the book of John. This includes the account of Jesus' life, death, and resurrection, and simultaneously reflects back to the beginning of the Bible. Next, read the remainder of the New Testament. By reading the New Testament first, you are better positioned to understand where the Old Testament is headed when you decide to tackle that part.

Follow Along with an Audio Bible Reading

Another helpful strategy is to follow along with an audio reading of the Bible. Many online Bible resources offer free Scripture reading. When you listen to someone else pronounce problematic names, the names become more memorable and accessible for future reading. Additionally, an audio version of the Bible may enhance your perception of the text as you hear the reader's voice inflections. The words on the page come alive through the reader's voice. Finally, some people find that following along to an audio Bible reading improves their ability to attend and absorb the text.

I enjoy listening to audio Scripture reading. Sometimes, I read and follow along in my Bible. Other times, I listen while driving, doing chores, or as I'm falling asleep. Listening to audio Bible reading is another valuable tool I employ to saturate my heart and mind with God's Word. I hope you consider availing yourself of this beneficial technique.

Connecting with God through Scripture nourishes our souls like no other book. I hope these strategies aid you in Bible reading. I pray you discover a bountiful harvest as you read the Bible and meet with the Author of truth and love.

Appendix C

Bible-Based Prayer

HAVE YOU EVER felt at a loss for words when praying? Or have you ever felt like your prayers have grown stale and dry?

The most powerful way I have found to strengthen and reignite my prayers is through Scripture. Below are some recommendations for enhancing your prayer life through Bible-based prayer.

Reading the Psalms Aloud

One of the easiest methods for incorporating Scripture into your prayers is by reading the Psalms aloud. The Psalms were originally written as songs and sung by God's people in worship, repentance, petition, and praise.

Begin by asking God to help you pray and focus on Him as you read the Scriptures. I recommend reading the given Psalm aloud when utilizing it in personal prayer. Reading Scripture out loud enables you to hear your own voice. This reminds you prayer is a conversation with God.

In addition, reading aloud slows down your reading tempo, so you can reflect more deeply on the words being spoken in prayer. This way, you can also pause and meditate on verses that resonate with you. Reading aloud slowly opens time and space for the Holy Spirit to highlight Scriptures that uniquely address your present circumstances. God communicates peace, comfort, hope, strength, conviction, love, and more through a prayerful reading of Scripture.

One area that requires explanation is verses about enemies in the Psalms. David was one of the Psalm writers. David led the

Israelites in many battles before and during his appointment as King of Israel. At times David was the enemy's sole target. The enemies were real and their purpose was to end his life or the lives of his people.

Therefore, when you come across verses about defeating enemies in the Psalms, you must frame this within the context of actual life-and-death situations. The psalmists brought these heartfelt petitions before the Lord because they needed God to save their lives.

Although many of us are not in a war zone or the intended target of a military operation, Satan is our enemy. He and his demonic forces are real. In John 10:10 (ESV) Jesus said, "The thief comes only to steal and kill and destroy. I came that they may have life and have it abundantly."

Consequently, when I am praying the Psalms aloud and come to verses asking God to defeat my enemies, I pray against enemies in the spiritual realm, just as David prayed against enemies in the physical realm. Similarly, when Jesus taught the Lord's Prayer, or Model Prayer, He included this statement: "And lead us not into temptation, but deliver us from evil" (Matt. 11:13, ESV). These verses about enemies and evil remind us we are in a serious spiritual battle. We need God's protection on every front.

The Psalms are filled with praise, thanksgiving, confession, worship, and petition. From the highest tribute to God to the lowest groan of pain, every emotion is expressed in the Psalms. Therefore, any emotion you may feel is articulated in the Psalms and will help you pray authentically.

When I read the Psalms aloud for personal prayer, I am astonished at how deeply this impacts my prayer time and brings the Scriptures to life. The most important points to remember are to read the Psalms out loud and give yourself time to read slowly, from the heart.

Bible-based Personal Prayers

Another effective technique for bolstering prayers through Scripture is to write the meaning of a Bible verse in your own words and then form that into a prayer.

Begin by collecting Bible verses that are meaningful to you. As discussed previously, be sure all verses are read in context.

Perhaps you need encouragement or peace that can only come from God. Search for Scriptures that address that topic. I recommend writing that verse in a notebook or on a notecard, or creating a document on your computer. Remember that the act of physically writing out a Bible verse etches it deeper in your memory.

Once the verse is recorded, ask God to help you capture the meaning of the verse in your own words. Then utilize those words to form a Scripture prayer.

Here are two examples:

1. ***Scripture of encouragement:*** "When you pass through the waters, I will be with you; and through the rivers, they shall not overwhelm you; when you walk through fire you shall not be burned, and the flame shall not consume you" (Isa. 43:2, ESV).

   Prayer in my own words, based on the meaning of this verse: Lord, thank You that no matter what I'm going through, You are with me. You will lift me up and shield me. Even in the most difficult times, I have nothing to fear. For You are my God. You are my hope and my salvation.

2. ***Scripture of peace:*** "Peace I leave with you; my peace I give to you. Not as the world gives do I give to you. Let not your hearts be troubled, neither let them be afraid" (John 14:27, ESV).

   Prayer in my own words, based on the meaning of this verse: Lord Jesus, I need Your peace. I receive Your peace. I rest in the peace You won for me at the cross. Nothing in the world can touch the love and grace You have given me. I place my faith and trust in You. I will not be afraid, for You are with me.

Like with the Psalms, I recommend reading the Scriptures and corresponding prayers aloud. Begin by reading the Bible verse out loud, because there is power in God's Word. Next, read aloud the corresponding prayer you have written.

You can keep these short Scripture prayers scattered around the house to help you reset your mind on God in prayer throughout the day. Additionally, you might assemble these Bible verses and corresponding prayers into a complete Bible-based prayer.

Elements to Include in a Full Scripture Prayer

There are many ways to structure a full prayer based on Bible verses. The elements I include when writing a complete Bible-based prayer are:

- *Praise:* Praise God for who He is. Praising God helps us remember God's greatness. Our problems shrink in light of His unmatched power and steadfast love.
- *Thanksgiving:* Thank God for what He has done through Christ. Thank God for the many blessings He has poured out. Thanking God rejuvenates our faith as we remember all the ways God has provided. Gratitude also softens our hearts so we can relate to God from a position of appreciation. We recall how much God loves us.
- *Confession and Repentance:* Confess any known sins and ask God's forgiveness. This removes pride or other sinful hindrances from interrupting our intimate relationship with God. We desire to approach Him with humility and honesty.
- *Petition or Requests:* Bring to God any needs, for yourself or for others. Our needs may be physical, emotional, or spiritual. No request is too small or too big for God.
- *Promises of God and Remembering His Strength:* A powerful way to end your prayers is with Bible verses about God's strength and promises. This refocuses our minds back on God and anchors our souls once again in Christ, who is our Rock of ages.

Example of a Complete Scripture Prayer

Using the method described above, I recorded Scripture verses and prayers on Post-It™ notes, forming an entire Bible-based prayer. This Scripture prayer guides my daily, personal prayer time. Through this Scripture prayer strategy, my prayers were amplified, my faith bolstered, and my heart connected more deeply with God.

Below is an example of a complete Scripture prayer or Bible-based prayer.

Praise

Scripture: "Yours, O Lord, is the greatness and the power and the glory and the victory and the majesty, for all that is in the heavens and in the earth is yours. Yours is the kingdom, O Lord, and you are exalted as head above all" (1 Chron. 29:11, ESV).

Corresponding Prayer: *O Lord, I praise Your mighty name. Everything in heaven and earth belongs to You. I see Your greatness in the stars above and in the beauty of the earth You have made. There is no one else like You. You rule and reign forever in glory, victory, and majesty. I join with creation singing, "Hallelujah!"*

Thanksgiving

Scripture: "Oh give thanks to the Lord, for he is good; for his steadfast love endures forever!" (Psalm 118:1, ESV).

Corresponding Prayer: *Thank you, Lord Jesus! You have proven Your goodness and love for me on the cross, where You died for my sins. Your mercy covers me forever. I am forgiven! Thank You for the countless earthly blessings, as well. For food, clean water to drink, clothing, shelter, a loving family and church family, a measure of health, and a job to earn money. Thank You for answering my prayers. Help me remember the blessings You have showered upon me through the years. You are good and Your mercy endures forever.*

Confession

Scripture: "If we confess our sins, he is faithful and just to forgive us our sins and to cleanse us from all unrighteousness" (1 John 1:9, ESV).

Corresponding Prayer: *Father God, I am sorry. Please forgive me for* [be specific]. *Thank you for cleansing me of sin as I repent and confess to You. Help me come before You with humility and honesty, knowing You see all and know all. You desire my eternal best. Strengthen me to become more like Christ in the beauty of holiness.*

Petitions or Requests

Scripture: "Do not be anxious about anything, but in every situation, by prayer and petition, with thanksgiving, present your requests to God" (Phil. 4:6, NIV).

Corresponding Prayer: *Lord God, I ask for Your help with my life and in the lives of my loved ones. I pray for healing, strength, and hope.* [Be specific for yourself and your loved ones.] *Draw me closer to Jesus by the power of Your Holy Spirit. Let Your Word come alive as I read. Help me be sensitive to the promptings of the Spirit. Empower me to speak and act like Jesus.*

Promises of God and Remembering His Strength

Scripture: "The steadfast love of the Lord never ceases; his mercies never come to an end; they are new every morning; great is your faithfulness" (Lam. 3:22–23, ESV).

Corresponding Prayer: *Father God, I rest in Your unconditional love. You are faithful and merciful. Come what may, I am safe in Your everlasting arms of love.*

My hope is these Bible-based prayer techniques will infuse your prayers with God's power, hope, truth, and love in ever-increasing measure. His Word endures forever. May we invite the Holy Spirit to weave God's Word into our words, so our prayers rise up with a fresh, heavenly fragrance and renew our vision of Christ.

Acknowledgments

I WANT TO EXPRESS my deepest gratitude to everyone who assisted me with this book.

Thank you to:

- My readers, who support me, read my work, and pray for me.
- My literary agent, Dave Fessenden of WordWise Media Services, for believing in this book and carrying out every element with excellence, wisdom, integrity, humor, and faith.
- The team at CLC Publications, for editing, publishing, and getting behind this book, and for sharing the good news of Christ with all nations.
- Ava Pennington, Amanda Roque, Marlene Bagnull, Teri Helm, Rev. Dr. Ed Crenshaw, and Emily Benco for coaching, assistance, and encouragement to answer God's call to write.
- The many Christian writers who uplift me and inspire me.
- Those who wrote endorsements and cheered me on.
- Kim Clark, for the author's photo.
- Everyone who prayed for me from beginning to end.
- My church family, for their prayers and love.
- My parents, who love me and taught me to love Jesus.
- My children and family, who love me always.
- My beloved husband, whose faithfulness, love, and support undergird my life.
- Most of all, thank You to my Lord and Savior, Jesus Christ, who makes all things possible.

Acknowledgments

Free Small-Group Study Guide Available!

Use the QR code or the link below to download Melissa McLaughlin's small-group study guide in PDF format. Feel free to make copies for everyone in your study group.

www.clcpublications.com/shop/the-whole-bible-devotional

This book is published by CLC Publications, an outreach of CLC Ministries International. The purpose of CLC is to make evangelical Christian literature available to all nations so that people may come to faith and maturity in the Lord Jesus Christ. We hope this book has been life changing and has enriched your walk with God through the work of the Holy Spirit. If you would like to know more about CLC, we invite you to visit our website:

www.clcusa.org

To know more about the remarkable story of the founding of CLC International we encourage you to read

LEAP OF FAITH

Norman Grubb

Paperback
Size 5¼ x 8, Pages 248
ISBN: 978-0-87508-650-7
ISBN (*e-book*): 978-1-61958-055-8

Also from CLC Publications

Unique Insight

Seeing Scripture from an Autistic Point of View

"Love the Lord your God with . . . all your mind" (Matt 22:37).
But what if your mind processes differently?

The Bible can be difficult to understand, but for people with autism spectrum disorder, it can be an even greater challenge. Its abstract, indirect, and subtle expressions and numerous allegories, metaphors, and satirical elements can be significant hurdles for those on the spectrum to comprehend. The Bible's intricate psychological, social, and emotional situations add further complexity.

Dr. Stella Pak, a physician specializing in adult neurology, understands these difficulties, being on the autism spectrum herself. "I prayed for divine wisdom to guide me in understanding His Word so that I could know who He is. He granted me the strength and patience to dive deep into the Scriptures. Through practice, I developed a skill set that allowed me to translate abstract scriptural concepts into concrete, relatable terms."

Her methods are not just geared to those on the autism spectrum but to anyone seeking a deeper understanding of biblical passages. Enrich your study of the Scriptures while cultivating a more inclusive and supportive environment for autistic Christians within your church community.

Paperback
Size 5.25 x 8, Pages 272
ISBN 978-1-61958-398-6
ISBN (*e-book*) 978-1-61958-399-3